PAIN KILLER MARKETING

HOW TO TURN CUSTOMER PAIN
INTO MARKET GAIN

PAIN KILLER MARKETING
HOW TO TURN CUSTOMER PAIN INTO MARKET GAIN

CHRIS STIEHL & HENRY J. DEVRIES

WBusiness Books

an imprint of New Win Publishing
a division of Academic Learning Company, LLC

ISBN 10: 0-8329-5016-5

ISBN 13: 978-0-8329-5016-2

Printed in the United States of America

First Edition

12 11 10 09 08   1 2 3 4 5

Library of Congress Cataloging-in-Publication Data

Stiehl, Chris.

   Pain-killer marketing : how to turn customer pain into market gain / by Chris Stiehl and Henry J. DeVries.

      p. cm.

   Includes bibliographical references.

   ISBN 978-0-8329-5016-2

   1. Analgesics industry--Marketing. I. DeVries, Henry. II. Title.

   HD9675.A442S74 2008

   615'.7830688--dc22

                                 2008005751

CONTENTS

FOREWORD

As a venture capitalist, I get pitched dozens of times every year, and almost every pitch contains "market research" lies. There are two types of market research lies: First, "facts" that "prove" that a market is big. Second, "our beta sites and focus groups told us they see a need for what we are doing."

I am often accused of ridiculing market research and focus groups. Guilty as charged. Please: Who makes important life decisions by inviting twelve strangers (often college students) in a room for a chat? However, I am not anti market research. My enemy is just bad market research.

My mission is to empower entrepreneurs. For them, I advocate real-world market research, a technique practiced by Honda, Wal-Mart, Dupont, and other successful companies that entails sending employees at every level to observe how their products or services are actually used by customers. What a concept, huh?

Two people who concur are Chris Stiehl and Henry DeVries, the self-proclaimed market research revolutionaries who wrote *Pain Killer Marketing.* I met Henry DeVries when I was researching my book *The Art of the Start.* Henry says he has never had an original idea in his life but owes his success to R & D: Rob and Duplicate. He researches great ideas and then encourages others to copy them.

This is a pragmatic book. It isn't a theoretical tome written by some academic (i.e., someone who can't do but can write and teach) or expert with war stories about what happened twenty years ago at General Motors when Kotler's Five Ps were the rage. The authors are market research contrarians who are in the trenches today with companies like Cisco, Palm and Johnson & Johnson.

If you're an entrepreneur creating version 1.0, the first time an expert tells you that you need to run your concept past focus groups, flee the scene as fast as you can. For your enjoyment, here's a list of the top ten things that you might find interesting about the book and its authors:

1. **Down with focus groups.** Focus groups rank as the number one waste of marketing research dollars.

2. **Ask to get.** If you want to know what customers think, go have conversations with them.

3. **Talk, don't survey.** One-on-one interviews do a better job than focus groups at uncovering customer pains, at a fraction of the cost. You don't need to survey hundreds or thousands. A dozen one-on-one interviews will generate as many customer pain points as seven focus groups.

4. **Shut up and listen up.** Companies that spend $50,000 on focus groups could obtain the same customer pains for under $5,000— and probably for free. But you have to learn how to listen.

5. **Reach out and touch someone by phone.** One-on-one interviews can be conducted by telephone as well – something difficult to achieve with focus groups if customers are spread out in different time zones.

6. **Go deep.** The depth of information obtained for each topic is actually greater in one-on-ones as well, since the moderator or facilitator does not feel the pressure to cover every topic.

7. **Find the pain.** Psychologists and sociologists have repeatedly found that consumers are more motivated to avoid pain than to seek pleasure. This book provides a proven method to find the pain of the customer and then "kill the pain" in sales and marketing messages.

8. **Skip the politicking.** How does a company decide which pain points to address? In most cases, the decisions are political, based upon who complains the loudest. Real world market research can help you decide what needs attention, how to select the appropriate issues, and what strategies would address the most pain points where you have the most to gain.

9. **A fact about co-author Chris Stiehl not in the book.** While playing baseball for UC San Diego, he set a collegiate record that can only be tied but never broken: he faced five batters and gave up 2 grand slam homeruns.

10. **A fact about Henry DeVries not in the book.** He came within one question of winning $13,000 on the TV game show *Jeopardy!* (but did manage to snag $13,000 on *Family Feud*).

The idea of changing the world is irresistible to entrepreneurs and to frustrated employees in many a moribund company. Go talk to a dozen customers or potential prospects. Ask good questions and then shut up and listen. Understand their FUD: fear, uncertainty and doubt. Then start prototyping and stop researching.

Guy Kawasaki
Founder of Alltop and Truemors
Co-Founder of Garage Technology Ventures
Author of *The Art of the Start*

ACKNOWLEDGEMENTS

We would like to thank our wives and families for supporting this effort and supporting us. There are many people who influenced this work, including Bradley Gale, W. Edwards Deming, Ray Kordupleski, Bob Klein, and Mel Klein for Mr. Stiehl. All five of these gentlemen spent significant hours training and teaching Mr. Stiehl how to find the answers to his questions about making a business customer-centric and profitable. John Schumann and Jim Dunn of The Whetstone Group were particularly helpful with the notions of using the concept of pain in the selling process. The teachings and writings of Dr. David Maister, Dr. Alan Weiss, and Dr. Glen Broom were of great value for Mr. DeVries, as was the writing of the late David Sandler, founder of the Sandler Sales Institute, and Michael Gerber, founder of the E-Myth Academy. We would also like to thank our clients for providing the real world problems that led to the discoveries we detail in the pages that follow, from General Motors and Pacific Gas & Electric Company to Silicon Valley stalwarts Palm and Cisco Systems. A final word of thanks to Art Chou and his tremendous team at WBusiness Books. It means so much to have true professionals in your corner.

INTRODUCTION

The Pain Killer Marketing Riddle

How will customers buy unless they trust you?

How, in turn, will they trust a person they have not heard?

How, in turn, will they hear without someone to speak?

How, in turn, will you speak unless you have a solution?

How, in turn, will you have a solution unless you understand their pain?

How will you understand their pain unless you listen?

1 Are You Into Pain?

"People don't care what you know, until they know that
you care."

OLD ADAGE

Did you know that psychologists and sociologists have repeatedly found that people are more motivated to avoid pain than to seek pleasure?

For instance, in an attempt to explain how and why some individuals with pain develop chronic-pain syndrome, in 1983, Letham et al introduced a so-called 'fear-avoidance' model. The central concept of their model is fear of pain. 'Confrontation' and 'avoidance' are postulated as the two extreme responses to this fear, of which the former leads to the reduction of fear over time. The latter, however, leads to the maintenance or exacerbation of fear, possibly generating a phobic state. An increasing number of investigations have corroborated and refined the fear-avoidance model.

Another example is that microeconomic theory maintains that purchases are driven by a combination of consumer preference and price. Knutson et al of Stanford University investigated how people weigh these factors and use pain to make purchasing decisions. These researchers demonstrated that separate parts of the brain are activated when people are confronted with financial gains versus financial losses. The study shows that distinct brain regions are triggered when consumers are offered products they wish to buy (a potential gain) and when they are offered the products' prices (representing a potential loss). The results of their study show that consumers are trading off the hoped-for gain of making a purchase against an immediate pain: the pain of paying money.[1]

Your target market experiences its own unique frustrations and pains. The secret to maximizing your attraction factor is to articulate the worries, frustrations, and concerns that you solve. As the old adage states, "People don't care what you know, until they know that you care." Truly identifying your market's predicament tells them that you understand and empathize with them.

Here are some ad headlines from companies who understand the power of pain:

- "What if your labeling printer makes 12,000 errors a minute?"
  —Zurich American Insurance

- "Here's to road warriors with spines of steel and delicate backs."
  —Courtyard by Marriott

- "Nickeled and dimed? I feel like I'm being quartered."
  —Charles Schwab

- "Is your cholesterol out of whack?"
  —Crestor by AstraZeneca

- "There's more at risk than your reputation."
  —Electro-Federation of Canada

- "We can't keep it from getting knocked around, but we can keep it from getting knocked out."
  —Tecra A8 Notebook Computer by Toshiba

- "Unburden your back."
  —Kensington Notebook Computer Cases

- "When bad vacations happen to good people."
  —Travel Guard International

If yours is a business that struggles with marketing, you are not alone. Many companies are tired of the rejection, frustration, and mystery of marketing.

There is a better way to attract customers. The secret is to turn their pain into your gain. Start by asking customers about their pains. Then gather information on how to solve those worries, frustrations, and concerns.

Let us ask you this (now, be honest): Do you really understand the problems of your prospects and customers? Or do you just think you know? Make no doubt about it, the stakes are high. Wrong marketing messages will cost you potential customers and lead to more struggles and frustration.

So here's how to become a new-customer magnet. Each group of prospects experiences its own unique frustrations and pains. What's the secret to crafting a marketing message that will maximize your attraction factor? Ask them (or have someone ask for you) about their pains. Start by asking a sample about their ideal business, and then segue into problems. Listen carefully to the exact words they use; you will want to mimic them in your marketing messages.

When you interview some current, past, and potential customers about the pains you solve, here are ten questions you should always ask:

1. Describe for me the "ideal" experience with a _____ (your product or service). How do most compare to this ideal?

2. Describe for me a recent time that the experience was less than ideal.

3. What are the three most important aspects of doing business with a _____.

4. If I said a _____ was a good value, what would that mean to you?

5. In what ways does dealing with a _____ cost you besides money (time, hassle, effort, etc.)?

6. What is the biggest pain about working with a _____?

7. Would you recommend a _____ to a friend or colleague? Why, or why not?

8. How does working with a _____ help you make money?

9. What does a _____ do really well?

10. If you had the opportunity to work with a _____ again, would you? Why, or why not?

This book is divided into two sections. In this first section we will lead you through the whys and the wherefores of what we call "Pain of Customer" research. In the second section we will explain how to apply your customers' pains to receive optimal marketing results.

A Checklist of Lessons Learned

1. Psychologists and sociologists have repeatedly found that customers are more motivated to avoid pain than to seek pleasure.
2. The secret to maximizing your attraction factor is to articulate the worries, frustrations, and concerns that you solve.
3. Interview some current, past, and potential customers about the pains you solve or want to solve.

2 The Big Equation of Business

As Brad Gale once asked, "Why should your customers give you money?"[1]

How Do You Define Your Business?

A brash market researcher at General Motors once asked a group of vice presidents, "What business are we in?"

The executives went along with the game and said GM was in the business of "designing, engineering, manufacturing, marketing, and selling automobiles."

"No!" said the market researcher, "We are in the transportation business. If you don't fully understand that, you won't see the threats." As he said this, the market researcher held up a copy of *Air Progress* from February 1971. The cover showed a man-sized affordable helicopter, à la Maxwell Smart from the TV show *Get Smart.*

One of the vice presidents in the room admitted that the railroad companies did not invest in the airline industry because they thought they were in the railroad business. They forgot that they were in the *transportation* business.

A similar exchange happened at Pacific Gas & Electric Company. A market researcher asked a group of vice presidents, "What business are we in?"

These executives answered that PG&E was in the business of "generating, transmitting, distributing, and delivering electricity and gas."

"No!" said the market researcher, "We are in the lighting, heating, and cooling business."

Again, the vice presidents were not defining the business in terms of the customer needs and pains that they satisfied. They did not see Toyota as a threat. Toyota was working on small-fuel-cell technology for use in trucks and automobiles.[2]

"Ah, but what if you put one of these fuel cells in your neighborhood and unplugged from the grid?" the market researcher asked. The executives did not have a good answer.

This book proposes that the pains and needs of the customer can be connected to not only marketing but all aspects of business improvement: metrics of success, customer feedback, and improvement initiatives. The Big Equation of Business, illustrates how this connectivity relates to making money. This equation was created by Bradley Gale, one of the gurus of quality in the United States. Dr. Gale was one of the experts involved in creating the Malcolm Baldrige National Quality Award in the late 1980s. His book, *Managing Customer Value*[3], is a must-read on the subject of using customer data to create value and profits.

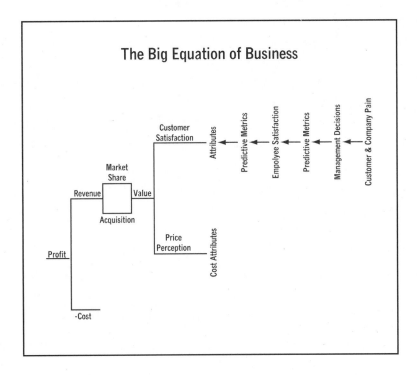

The Big Equation of Business

The Big Equation of Business

We begin with the Big Equation of Business on the left side. Marketing 101 teaches that Profits are determined by Revenue minus Cost. We will not discuss cost at this point, except to point out that, as with the fresh-popcorn example (see Chapter 4), understanding customer needs and pains can lead to saving money.

If we now focus on Revenue, this comes from Market Share and Acquisitions of new markets or of Market Share (buying your way into a new market or market segment). What drives Market Share? Dr. Gale preaches that the answer to that question is the customer perception of Value, not just price[4].

During workshops we illustrate this by asking the audience, "Who here drives a used Yugo?" If no hands go up, then the answer obviously is that more than price is considered in the purchase of an automobile, because a used Yugo is the cheapest car. Dr. Gale's premise is that customers look at the total deal: What do I get and what am I going to pay for it? If there are three soups at the grocery store: store brand, Progresso, and Campbell's, you may buy the store brand or you may buy one of the others if you had a coupon or it was on sale. You would evaluate the deal. He talks about "fair value" comparisons: high quality at a high price and lower quality at a lower price. Companies that want to gain in market share should strive to have high quality at a lower price.

What drives a high-value perception? Value equals what you get (quality + service + reputation) divided by what you give up (money + hassle + time + whatever). The idea is that the customer picks the best overall deal for the money, not just based upon price alone, but the best deal.

Value is predicted by customer satisfaction (perception of quality) AND price perception (NOT just price, but all price attributes — e.g., cost, hassle factor, how tough you are to do business with, customer service, etc.).

Depending upon what the analysis (e.g., the House of Quality — see

Chapter 15) is built to include, any or all of these factors may be in there. The attributes analysis usually excludes price issues because they tend to overwhelm everything else. The job of the "Internal Predictive Metrics" is to predict what will have the most impact on Customer Satisfaction. In so doing, they predict what will ADD to the perception of value.

If something is an expected and necessary part of the transaction (see Chapter 12 concerning the Kano Model), then that being lacking would predict Customer Dissatisfaction and lower perception of value.

The Big Equation of Business suggests that the value perception is driven by the perception of quality (Customer Satisfaction) and the perception of price. Many companies have a customer-satisfaction survey, but few of them are based upon a well-articulated "Pain of the Customer" (more on this in a later chapter). Do you have a well-articulated list of customer price attributes? Price has more than one component! How easy is it to do business with you? How easy is it to get help if help is needed? How knowledgeable is your sales staff? How easy is it to use and understand your product or service? Very few companies research and collect the customer price attributes.

As will be shown in the Customer-Driven Model of Improvement (see Chapter 4), the internal predictive metrics for the business need to be linked to the "Pain of the Customer." These metrics are predictive of success with Customer Satisfaction. What predicts success with the internal predictive metrics? The answer here is that the employees drive success with the metrics. If you manage a call center, for example, and your internal metric is "Number of Calls Handled," that does not lead to appropriate employee behavior. Why? Customers wind up feeling rushed. The employee wants to hurry and get to the next call in the queue. This leads to customer dissatisfaction. It also leads to employee dissatisfaction, as they know they are not completely meeting the customer's needs.

If your metric is "Average time for a call where first-call satisfaction is guaranteed," then this would lead to employees trying to make sure all the customer needs are met, and trying to do that faster over time. Here is an example of a call center for a technology company using the "Number of Calls" metric where a rework measure was implemented. Customers waiting in the queue were asked if they had ever called about their problem before. As many as 40% had called once or more about the same problem. That is a lot of rework! If "First-Call Satisfaction" were the metric, all of those calls would disappear from the queue. The employees and customers would both feel better about the call.

Do you have a well-articulated "Pain of the Employee" study? Do you have predictive metrics for employee satisfaction? An upcoming chapter will deal with the issue of researching employee satisfaction. Do you ask employees what management wants to know, or what employees want to say? Most companies ask questions composed by and for the management on their employee-satisfaction surveys. Very few companies conduct "Pain of the Employee" studies, treating the employees as "customers" of the metrics and policies derived by management.

Once the pain of the customer, the pain of the employee, and the company pain (growth, product development, lack of profits, etc.) are identified via the methods outlined in other chapters (e.g., Chapter 4), then management makes decisions and sets actions in motion that affect the rest of the Big Equation of Business. Much like successive runners pass the baton on to subsequent team members, in an ideal customer-centric company, the pains of the company and the customers drive decisions that lead to greater profits, as outlined in the Big Equation of Business.

Thus, the Big Equation of Business demonstrates the linkages needed from management decision-making through employee-performance metrics to customer satisfaction and profits. Have you established all of these linkages? Have you executed the necessary research?

In the next chapter (the "Movie Theater" chapter), we will talk about a small-town movie-theater owner and his struggle to meet customer needs and solve their pains. One of the key features of this owner's approach was that he was able to rethink his definition of the business. He was able to realize that he needed to define his business in terms of the customer needs that his theater met. This is a good object lesson for any business: Can you define your business in terms of the customer needs that you satisfy or pains that you solve?

A Checklist of Lessons Learned

1. You should be able to define your business in terms of the customer needs you meet or the pains you solve for the customer. The definition of your business starts with the customer.

2. The Big Equation of Business illustrates the way that all parts of the business are linked to each other, from management vision and decision-making to profits.

3. You need to establish the linkages in the equation. They will be there anyway, but if you do not establish and manage these linkages, you will not maximize profits.

4. Make sure the "Pain of the Customer" is deployed throughout the organization, and the customer stays in the room when decisions are made.

SECTION ONE:
FINDING THE PAIN OF THE CUSTOMER

3 The Small-Town-Movie Theater Example

As Yogi Berra once said, "Nobody goes there; it's too crowded!"[1]

Let's Play a Game

Suppose for a moment that you own a small-town movie theater. A theater built in the 1930s or so, with a stage below the screen. This was the theater where all the neighborhood kids would go in the 1950s to see the matinees and the *Buck Rogers* or *Superman* serials. The balcony has been redesigned so that the theater now has two screens and shows two movies at a time. Who is the competition? The mega-mall theater a couple of miles away is much more modern, with about 12 screens and better parking.

Further suppose that you and your significant other are going away to Europe for a couple of weeks. If you have ever owned a small business, you know how difficult this would be to achieve a meaningful vacation. Most small-business owners spend every waking hour thinking about their business while keeping it afloat.

You decide to leave your assistant manager in charge. While you are away, you want a one-page fax waiting for you at each hotel telling you how the business is running while you are away. You are not taking your cell phone or your laptop. You want to really feel free. So, only your key dashboard metrics will be on this fax. Take out a sheet of paper and write down what you might want to know while you are away. Remember, you only get one page. It is expensive to fax to Europe.

Do not read on until you have made your list.

Many items are mentioned frequently. Audiences vary a little, but most groups mention many of the items shown in Table 1 below.

Table 1: Theater Owner Metric List
Attendance (broken down by time & screen)
Gross Revenue (broken down by tickets & concessions)
Employee Issues (everyone show up & on time?)
Expense, Costs or Bills Received
Customer Complaints
Movie News (general & local)
Neighborhood News (bad & good)
Building Issues (maintenance, etc.)
Weather Issues

Let's Change the Game

You no longer own the movie theater. In this scenario, it is Friday night and you and your significant other are at dinner. You decide to go to the movies. You agree on a movie. (This would be a major miracle in most homes. It would probably have to be an Arnold Schwarzenegger romantic comedy. *True Lies* was the perfect movie for many households.)

The movie is showing at two different theaters nearby. The start times, admission prices, and distances to the theaters are not at issue. How would you decide which theater to visit?

As before, make a list of what might be important factors for you and your significant other in deciding where to see the movies before looking at Table 2.

Audiences typically find this list much easier to generate. The list shown in Table 2 captures the ten items most frequently mentioned as a reason to choose one theater over another.

Write your list down, then turn the page and see if our typical audience responses agree with you.

Table 2: Movie Goer Needs List
Clean Floors (not sticky)
Clean Bathrooms
Best Food (fresh popcorn!)
Stadium Seating
Cup Holders
Less Crowded
Fewer Teen-agers
Easy Parking
Neighborhood Issues (crime, etc.)

Why Don't the Lists Agree?!

Should they agree? It appears that what customers are using to vote with their feet and their dollars is not being tracked by the company! Again, the first list was a "good" list, but it lacked customer-centric metrics and was looking backward in time. The second list, the customer list, includes many things that can be anticipated (cleanliness, fresh popcorn, etc.) and measured in a *predictive* way. Do you believe that there are customer pains associated with movie-theater experiences relating to each of these statements in Table 2? The idea would be to adapt the owner list to incorporate some of these customer metrics, to make sure that pain is not experienced by the owner's customers.

Let's examine both lists and look for meaningful traits.

One key characteristic of the items that typically show up on the owner's list (Table 1) is that they tend to be bottom-line oriented and tend to look backward in time. Even with Fortune 500 companies, the company dashboard tends to look very similar. The first five items in the list (down through "complaints") are mentioned by almost every group. The latter five issues appear occasionally, but infrequently. Rarely is there a customer-oriented metric. If there is one, it is often "complaints." Once a customer complains, several others may have walked out of the theater with the same experience without mentioning it. It is too late. If any of these metrics looked bad while you were in Europe, how would you know what to do? This is a "good" list for many businesses, but it can be improved.

The items on the customer list (Table 2) are often items that can be anticipated. The movie-theater owner can design metrics to predict how the customers are going to feel about these issues, by recognizing the pain that they represent from the customers' pasts. For example, while you are in Europe, you could ask how often the bathrooms and floors were cleaned. How often did you dump out the popcorn and pop it fresh?

If the customer list is what is being used to decide where the money and people go, then the business probably should have metrics off this list among those on the business dashboard. Some of these may seem to be difficult to control, such as the perceived level of crime in the neighborhood. Others are easily converted to predictive metrics (such as, how fresh is the popcorn? If it is less than ten-minutes old, the customer is likely to say it is fresh — more on this in the next chapter).

Developing Predictive Customer-Centric Metrics for Your Business

One of the key messages of this book is that you should be able to define your business in terms of the customer pains and needs that you solve. Learning how to listen to customers, how to develop the "Pain of the Customer," is the best way to make sure this is accomplished. The Movie-Theater Example illustrates how easy it is to stop thinking like a customer when you are in business, how easy it is to develop your business metrics without having customer-centric metrics on your dashboard. It takes a concerted effort to develop predictive customer-centered metrics. These should predict positive outcomes in key areas of customer decision-making.

Of course, many companies have customer-satisfaction data on their dashboards as a customer-centric metric. This book will discuss ways to use this data later, but customer satisfaction data is NOT predictive. It tells you how well you dealt with the customers' pains and needs in the past, not now or in the future.

The next chapter discusses what the owner of the movie theater decided to do and measure, as well as how it worked.

A Checklist of Lessons Learned

1. Let the customer describe how they decide whether or not to buy your product or service in their own terms; don't assume you know what they want or what they fear (their potential pain). Make sure you ask!

2. Make certain that your business is tracking predictive metrics of success with customers, not just backwards-looking bottom-line-oriented metrics.

3. Learn how to think like a customer, even while you are inside the company; don't check your customer mentality at the door as you go to work.

4. You may need to invest in market research to develop target values for the customer-oriented metrics that you develop (e.g., how old can the popcorn be and still taste "fresh"?).

5. The customer-oriented metrics can enable you to know what to fix if your revenue metrics show poor performance. (If your attendance is down while you are in Europe, the customer-oriented metrics may be able to tell you where your assistant's performance is failing the business.)

4 Stale Popcorn into Fresh Popcorn

A strategic planning truism is "You get what you measure!"[1]

How Do Customers Decide?

The small-town theater exercise in the previous chapter was based on an actual theater in Michigan. If you visited that theater at 4:00 p.m. on a Friday, you would notice a high-school boy opening a bag of pre-popped popcorn as big as he was and dumping it into a large bin. By 8:00 p.m., this popcorn could be made warm and could be smothered in butter, but it was not likely to taste "fresh." This directly applies to one of the pains described by customers when they were asked how they picked a movie theater. The theater with freshly popped popcorn was likely to get more customers because their popcorn was fresh.

The movie-theater owner was throwing away a lot of stale popcorn at the end of each evening. His popcorn sales were not as strong as he had hoped.

Once this pain/need was identified in interviews, the practice was changed. A smaller bin was purchased, along with a small popper. A kitchen timer was purchased. Research was done over a couple of weekends to determine that ten minutes was the "taste lifetime" of popcorn—the time it was still considered to taste fresh by customers. The theater owner decided to pop popcorn almost continuously. The popcorn was thrown out every ten minutes, the kitchen timer was reset, and a new small batch was made.

Thus, when customers were coming into the theater they had an experience they had not had before: They could smell, hear, and see popcorn being popped fresh. What was the result? Popcorn sales skyrocketed. The amount thrown away each night went down, even though he was making a number of batches per night. Attendance began to rise. The owner made money on popcorn sales, he saved money by throwing away less, and ticket sales increased.

The Customer-Driven Improvement Model

The model used by the movie-theater owner is illustrated below. This may be one of the most important ideas in this book: Your business metrics, customer satisfaction surveys, and improvement initiatives should all be based upon and rooted in the "Voice/Pain of the Customer." There should be conscious connections between these functions. This point will be demonstrated several times throughout the book in various examples.

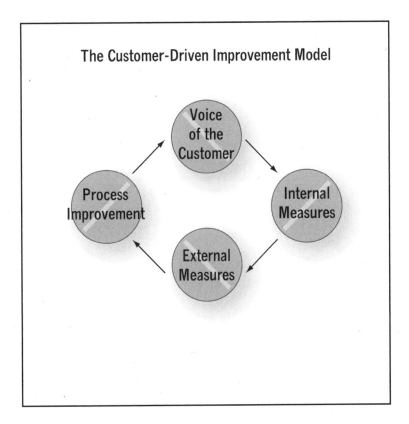

The first step, determining the "Voice/Pain of the Customer," represents qualitative research. This will be discussed in some detail in the next chapter.

The second step is the development of predictive internal metrics. We have subsequent chapters on how this difficult task is done. The external measures represent customer-satisfaction surveys. These also are discussed later, but the idea is that the customers essentially define what should be in the survey by describing their wants, needs, and pains. Finally, the process improvements and initiatives should be linked to the previous steps. It makes no difference what process-improvement methodology is chosen (Deming, Juran, Crosby, DMAIC, Six Sigma—see references). All of these approaches use the customer pains, wants, and needs as the foundation of their program.

So, how was this model used by the movie-theater owner? The diagram below shows the fresh-popcorn example mapped into this model.

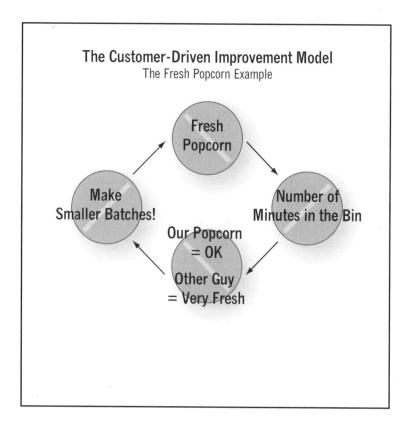

The owner was able to link the customer "Pain " (stale popcorn is bad, fresh popcorn is good) to a predictive internal metric (if the popcorn is less than ten minutes old, it is considered fresh by the customer). The customer data told him that what he was doing now (pre-popped popcorn spending hours in the bin) was not working. He decided to implement a process change. He made a new batch of popcorn every ten minutes. Popcorn sales improved, costs were reduced (he threw away less) and his attendance increased.

A Checklist of Lessons Learned

1. When you link your metrics and improvement initiatives to meeting the customer's needs and eliminating their pain, the results can be unparalleled.

2. Your customer research and customer-satisfaction surveys should be directed at solving the customer's pain and meeting their needs; i.e., determining the target values for predictive internal metrics.

3. Using the Customer-Driven Improvement Model ensures that the "Pain of the Customer" is deployed throughout the organization, and the customer stays in the room when decisions are made.

5 Who Else Wants to Turn Client Pain into Marketing Gain?

As Yogi Berra once said, "You've got to be careful if you don't know where you are going, because you might not get there."[1]

Pain Killer Marketing isn't just for product and service companies. This also works for consultants looking for clients - both internal and external consultants.

If you are a consultant who is a little frustrated about how to attract enough clients, you are not alone. Many consultants struggle with marketing and hope that networking will bring them enough clients. This isn't exactly hoping and wishing for clients, but it is darn close.

There is a better way to get clients. First you probe for pain, then you educate prospects on how to solve their pains in general. The more you educate how to solve their pain in general, the more that will engage you for specific consulting advice.

Unfortunately, many consultants who learn this truth find the idea of writing and speaking about customer pain too daunting and even mysterious. Most feel this is only for a select few mega-minds like Peter Drucker, Suze Orman, or Tom Peters, but that is a miscalculated view. You don't need to write three dozen books and have them translated into thirty languages. Just becoming a local guru can work wonders, both within the company and within your geographical area.

Consulting is what economists sometimes call "credence" goods, in that purchasers must place great faith in those who sell the services. How can potential clients trust you if they never hear what you have to say?

The good news is there exists a body of knowledge that some have discovered to grow their consulting business. As an example, management-consulting firms like McKinsey & Co. pioneered the approach beginning in the

1940s[2] and now have it down to a science.

How do you get started as a guru? First, understand that generating new clients is an investment and should be measured like any other investment. Next, quit wasting money on ineffective means like brochures, advertising, and sponsorships. Rather than creating a brochure, start by writing "how-to" articles. Those articles turn into speeches and seminars. The best marketing investment you can make is to get help creating informative Web sites, hosting persuasive seminars, booking speaking engagements, and getting published as a newsletter columnist and eventually, a book author.

Please know this: The universe rewards activity. Start by being curious and asking clients about their pains. Gather information on how to solve those worries, frustrations, and concerns. Be the expert who educates people on how they compare to their peers and the best ways to overcome their obstacles.

A Checklist of Lessons Learned

1. You must be heard and recognized as an expert in the customers' (or the clients') pains in order to succeed as a consultant.

2. There are proven steps and strategies to pursue to achieve guru status.

6 How to Attract All the Customers You Need

In the words of motivational speaker Zig Ziglar: "You can get whatever you want in life if you just help enough people get what they want."

In his 1954 classic book *The Practice of Management*, business visionary Peter Drucker said, "There is only one valid definition of business purpose: to create a customer." To do this, a business must answer three classic questions: What is our business? Who is our customer? What does our customer consider valuable?

The number-one challenge for any organization is creating new customers. However, many companies feel marketing is too time-consuming, expensive, or undignified. Even if they try a marketing or business development program, most companies are frustrated by a lack of results. They even worry if marketing would ever work for them. And no wonder. According to Dr. David Maister, a former professor from Harvard Business School, the typical sales and marketing hype that works for retailers and manufacturers is not only a waste of time and money for companies, it actually makes them less attractive to prospective customers.

However, research has proven there is a better way. There is a proven process for marketing with integrity and getting an up-to 400% to 2,000% return on your marketing investment (detailed by DeVries and Bryson in the book *Client Seduction*). At the New-Client Marketing Institute, coauthor Henry DeVries calls it the Educating Expert Model, and the most successful professional service and consulting firms use it to get more customers than they can handle. Internal consultants can use these techniques within companies to garner clients and support. We think the approach has implications for almost all service and product businesses too.

To attract new customers, the best approach is to demonstrate your expertise by giving away valuable information through writing and speaking.

Unfortunately, many companies who learn this truth find the idea of writing and speaking too daunting and even mysterious. Most feel this is only for a select few like Bill Gates or Jack Welch, but that is a miscalculated view. In the beginning, it is not unusual to wonder how these other companies get in front of audiences and get their "how-to" advice in print.

What should you do to increase revenues? First, understand that generating leads is an investment and should be measured like any other investment. Next, quit wasting money on ineffective means like brochures, advertising and sponsorships. The best marketing investment you can make is to get help creating informative Web sites, hosting persuasive seminars, booking speaking engagements, and getting published as a newsletter columnist and, eventually, a book author.

Rather than creating a brochure, start by writing how-to articles. Those articles turn into speeches and seminars. Later, you gather the articles and publish a book through a strategy called print on demand self-publishing (we've seen it done in under ninety days and for less than a $1,000). Does it work? Following is a list of business best-seller titles that started out self-published[1]:

- *The One-Minute Manager,* by Kenneth Blanchard and Spencer Johnson: picked up by William Morrow & Co.

- *In Search of Excellence,* by Thomas Peters (of McKinsey & Co.): in its first year, sold more than twenty-five thousand copies directly to consumers — then Warner sold ten million more.

- *Leadership Secrets of Attila the Hun,* by Weiss Roberts: sold half a million copies before being picked up by Warner.

Even if you believe in the Educating Expert Model, how do you find time to do it and still get customer and admin work done? No business ever believes they have too much time on their hands. Nothing worth happening in business ever just happens. The answer is to buy out the time for marketing. You need to be involved, but you should not do this all on your own. Trial and error is too expensive of a learning method. Wouldn't it be better if someone helped you who knows the tricks and shortcuts? We can show you how to leverage your time and get others to do most of the work for you, even if you are a solo practitioner.

How much should you invest in marketing? That depends on your business goals, but here are some norms. Law firms generally spend about two percent of their gross revenues on marketing, and the average expenditure is about $136,000. Marketing costs for accounting firms average about seven to ten percent of gross revenue.[2] The typical architecture, engineering, planning, and environmental consulting firm spent a record 5.3 percent of their net service revenue on marketing.[3]

Does Pain-Killer Marketing work? Companies we have studied use this approach to increase revenues through more new customers, more fee income per customer, and more money from past customers. Here are just a few concrete examples:

- Through an informational Web site and electronic newsletter, one management consultant added an additional $100,000 in revenue from speaking engagements and sales of information products within two years.

- In forty-five days, a business that served the home-building industry was able to launch a Web site and education expert campaign that helped him double his business in a year.

- Using one strategy alone, a Web marketing agency was able to double income and add $100,000 of revenue in one year.

- By switching over to the model, a marketing-services company was able to receive a 2,000% return on investment of its new marketing campaign that featured how-to advice seminars and articles from senior executives.

- When an IT consulting company gave up cold calling and switched to this model, the quality of their leads dramatically improved and closed deals quickly increased by 25%.

- Using these strategies of seminars and getting published, a law-firm has grown in a few years from a regional practice to a national firm.

- A well-established regional-accounting-firm customer reported they were able to accomplish more in six months with these methods than they had in three years on their own.

- An advertising agency used the strategy to double revenues from $4.5 to $9.6 million in five years and earn a spot in the Ad Age 500.

- With this model a one-hundred-year-old financial-services firm was able to double awareness and create one hundred thousand qualified leads per year for its advisors.

Please know this: The universe rewards activity. Start by asking customers about their pains. Gather information on how to solve those worries, frustrations, and concerns. Be the expert who educates people on how they compare to their peers and the best ways to overcome their obstacles. The more prospects you inform how to solve their problems in general, the more will hire you for the specifics.

A Checklist of Lessons Learned

1. Whether you are an internal guru or a consultant, give away knowledge to build your reputation as the person who understands the customer's pain.

2. There are proven techniques that can translate into more customers and clients without investing inordinate amounts of time.

7 Why Worry About the Pain of the Customer?

Bradley Gale and Robert Buzzel stated, "...businesses with a superior product/service offering clearly outperform those with inferior quality."[1]

Does Worrying About the Customer's
Pain Really Pay Off?

The data from over 450 companies[2] shows that companies that care about quality and meeting customer needs have stronger customer loyalty (more repeat business) and are less vulnerable to pricing strategies (price wars). These companies can command higher prices for their products and services. They have lower marketing costs. A customer who buys from one of these companies is less likely to be challenged by management for making that decision. It is a "safe" decision.

Many companies collect pain points. We have seen lists of several hundred pain points within a division of a Fortune 500 company. How does this company decide which pain points to address? In most cases, the decisions are political, based upon who complains the loudest. Obviously, with a list of several hundred pain points, only a small percentage of these ever get attention. Much of the focus of this book is to help you decide what needs attention, how to select the appropriate issues and what strategies would address the most pain points where you have the most to gain.

As you progress through this book, realize that most customers respond to products and services that reduce their pain or their risk of pain. Do you remember the ads for headache and pain relievers from years ago? Some of these ads give you the impression that they are striving to create the headache that their product would then solve! Customers respond to pain in advertising. Any popular magazine illustrates this point. The ads, even in business magazines, often focus on one or more pain points and use the solution or reduction of pain as a key to the promotion of their product or service.

Keep in mind that the pain of the customer is the foundation of Pain Killer Marketing and all of the processes described herein.

An example of using the Pain of the Customer techniques to drive successful buzz marketing was the introduction of Palm devices a few years ago. To promote their usage among professionals, Palm gave away Palm Pilots at a conference preloaded with conference details and schedules. The conference attendees were given the opportunity to purchase the device at the end of the conference, at a discount from the retail price. Many of the conference attendees were so impressed with the device after a few days of usage that they were eager to purchase one. The marketing strategy resulted in tremendous "buzz" about the Palm device. Palm had solved the conference attendees' pain of not knowing what was happening and where in a convenient, easy-to-use format. The strategy generated hundreds of customer advocates among key professionals.

A Checklist of Lessons Learned

1. The pain of the customer is the foundation of much of his or her purchasing behavior—relieving pain or avoiding it.

2. Objectives drive design: Creating profits for your business is a process that finds a way to efficiently identify how to deal with the pain of the customer.

8 Collecting the Pain of the Customer

Recent research conducted by The Product Development and Management Association (PDMA) confirms that companies that gather and use Voice/Pain of the Customer information as part of a new product development process are more successful than those who don't.[1]

What is the "Pain of the Customer"?

Businesses have been studying their customers for eons. Remember the old Western movies or episodes of *Gunsmoke* on TV? Whenever a rider would come into town, he might ride up to the blacksmith, toss him a coin, and say, "Take care of my horse." The smithy knew what to do. He knew his customer's needs. He watered the horse, groomed the horse, checked the shoes and health of the horse—everything that the cowboy traveler would expect to be done. Similarly, in the 1950s, when you pulled into a "service station," an attendant would check your tires and oil, clean your windshield and rear window, and pump your gas.

Or take a company like Cadillac, for example, where the market-research library contains detailed research reports dating back to the 1920s. So, why has the notion of the "Voice/Pain of the Customer" gained so much prominence recently?

In the 1970s and 1980s, the Quality movement gained considerable attention, resulting in the creation of the Malcolm Baldrige National Quality Award in the U.S. in 1987.[2] The automotive industry studied how the Japanese manufacturers were gaining market share. Among other things, market researchers at General Motors noticed that Japanese automotive engineers were at the GM exhibit at Disney World's Epcot Center observing people interacting with GM cars. The Japanese engineers did not interact directly with the people, but just watched them and took notes. The Japanese were using GM facilities to study GM customers! While GM thought of Epcot as a marketing tool, the Japanese automakers thought of it as a research tool.

GM soon began to implement some of the Japanese methods. One of the first Quality Function Deployment teams[3] was at the Fisher Body Division of General Motors in 1982. GM began to link design specifications to the customer's wants, needs, and pains. Akashi Fukuhara, among others, provided instruction on how this was done. He had been a government official in Japan who retired and moved to Dearborn, Michigan[4]. While he was willing to teach, Fukuhara believed that companies in the United States would never have the patience or the discipline to execute the Japanese methodologies. He thought U.S. companies could only behave like John Wayne: Shoot first and ask questions later. To Fukuhara, we were all renegade cowboys.

John Hauser and others studied what U.S. automakers were doing in Detroit and composed the "House of Quality" article in the *Harvard Business Review*—among the most frequently requested reprints of *HBR*.[5] This was followed by Abbie Griffin's paper, "The Voice of the Customer" a few years later.[1] Although this paper outlined the most successful methodologies for executing Pain of the Customer studies, many market-research firms do not use the preferred proven methodologies, even today. The preferred methodologies create a Pain of the Customer in customer language, organized and prioritized by customers. What follows is a brief discussion of the Pain of the Customer Process. This process has been implemented successfully hundreds of times, including in companies such as Palm, Cisco Systems and LifeScan in recent years.

The Pain of the Customer Process

Phase 1 of the Pain of the Customer Process begins with a clear definition of who the target customers are and an "in-house" discussion of the issues and pains that are likely to be broached during an interview. Key customer contact personnel are included in discussions of each potential customer or customer group and their known key issues or pains.

An interview guide is written. The interview guide is primarily an exposition of known issues and probes, not to elicit solutions. The purpose of the interview guide is to represent all known issues. In any one interview, only a subset of these issues will be covered – those where the customer has the greatest passion. Thus, in a very real sense, the customer will direct or lead the conversation. The guide is used to make sure the interviewers have knowledge of all issues and potential probes to ask. As the interviews progress, the conversations can be directed toward issues that have not been as well developed as you would like. The key is to understand that this is qualitative research, so it is not important (perhaps not even desirable) for every respondent to answer every question. An example Interview Guide for the Movie Theater Example in Chapter 3 is shown below.

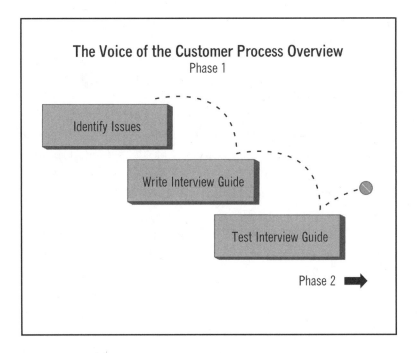

Interview Guide: Going to the Movies

My name is _____, and I would like to have a conversation with you about going to the movies. There are no right or wrong answers to the questions that I will ask. I really just want to know your opinions, OK?

1. How often do you go to the movies? Where do you go? Typically, with whom do you go? Tell me how you decide what movie to see and where to see it? Describe where you were the last time you had to decide this and how the conversation progressed?

2. What is important in deciding where to go? (Hints: friendliness of staff, parking, quality of food, typical attendees, etc.)

3. What would make you rule out a theater for consideration? Why?

4. What is it like, what are you thinking, as you approach the theater?

5. What is important about buying your tickets and getting into the theater? (Probes: comfort, speed, friendliness of staff, etc.)

6. Some people say the quality of the food is very important. What do you think?

7. What does it mean to have a "clean" theater?

8. What does "comfort" mean? (Hints: stadium seating, cup holders, reclining seats, etc.)

9. What is important about the sound and the screen? Why?

10. Where do you prefer to sit inside the theater?

11. When you leave, what is important?

12. What have I forgotten to ask you that I should have asked you?

13. Thank You for Your Time and Opinions

The passion that is displayed by the prospective customers in this qualitative phase can help you understand the market potential for your product or service.

Try to make every question as open-ended as you can, even to the point of being a little bit vague at the start, and then getting more and more specific as you explore a topic. The devil is in the details, but you don't want to miss any "big picture" ideas that they have. For example, you could ask something like "What prompts you to want to go to the movies?"—something kind of "big picture" regarding the issues at hand.

You need a "warm-up" question or two. Usually, for an industrial customer, we ask something like "Tell me about your responsibilities at _____. What are your major priorities?" Hopefully, the issue you are researching is among those priorities. If not, then ask "Where does <your issue> fit in your priorities? ...in your company's priorities?" The purpose of the warm-up is to get them talking about themselves, to relax them a little, to make them feel comfortable. Make it an easy question for them to answer. This part of the discussion should last five minutes or fewer.

You need probes. Market researchers call this aspect of the interview "Asking the five why's." You should probe up to five times with a "why" question to get to the need or detailed pain description. Some questions may involve "solution selling." Try something like "In other words, how helpful would it be to you to have a competent assessment of your <your issue> and what steps might assure your compliance? Why would that be helpful?" In this way, they will discuss some of their personal pain points that your company could solve. Their answers to this would provide great marketing material.

Other probes might include: When you ask about their problems, ask them how they deal with them now and how those problems affect them personally in their jobs. This is another way of eliciting the customers' pain.

Ask them how being found to NOT be satisfactory with your issue would affect their company. What would happen? How would the company's management feel about that? What pain would they experience? Remember, most people respond to the need to reduce, eliminate, or avoid pain. This is what you want to explore: What pain would they feel and what might it be worth to avoid that pain?

At the end, ask them where in the company's priorities the concerns that you have raised in the interview fall. Are they extremely important? Moderately important? Not even on the radar screen?

You always want to close by asking something like "What questions should I have asked you that I have left out? What is on your mind about this that we have not yet discussed?"

Always thank them profusely for their time and assistance at the end.

You should think about if you want to offer them any follow-up after your study is over. If so, you should mention that at closing. You may offer a memo summarizing some of the things you heard in your interviews. You may offer a follow-up telephone call in the future. They have given you their opinions. It is a good idea to offer them something in return (a company logo gift like a Cross pen, for example). They often want to know how the industry as a whole is viewing these issues—not naming any companies—but a general memo indicating that this may be a serious concern would be nice. This would be an opportunity to mention that you offer services as well.

Next, the interview guide is tested and reviewed with selected staff and, perhaps, a couple of customers who would be willing to give critical feedback. The testing is to make sure the issues are understood, the questions make sense, and the interviewer exhibits the proper interview techniques (active listening, etc.). All of this is accomplished before interviews are scheduled and conducted.

Phase 2 of the Pain of the Customer Process begins with the execution of the interviews. The interviews are conducted using a unique style and technique. Active listening plays a key role. The interview takes the direction of the passions of the customer. Even though an interview guide is developed with great care, the interview may not continue in the order of the guide. It may go in any direction, depending upon the passions of the customer. The guide begins with very general topics, and questions are developed exploring each detail of the product or service. However, it is rare that an interview covers all topics.

Research has shown[6] that fifteen to twenty one-on-one interviews conducted in this manner result in over 90% of the customers' wants, pains, and needs being generated, as compared to a dozen focus groups of ten to twelve customers each, at a lot less cost and effort, since the customers need not all be in the same place at the same time for one-on-one interviews. The research has shown that twelve to fifteen one-on-one interviews generate as many needs statements as seven focus groups! One-on-one interviews can be conducted by telephone as well—something difficult to achieve with focus groups if customers are spread out in different time zones. The depth of information obtained for each topic is actually greater in one-on-ones as well, since the moderator or facilitator does not feel the pressure to cover every topic, but rather wants to cover the topics that interest this particular customer in greater detail—their passions.

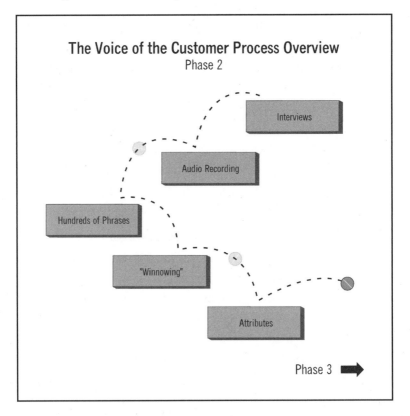

The interviews are recorded for analysis and to preserve the customer language. The interviews are analyzed to generate hundreds of phrases that contain pains, wants and needs (product or service attribute statements). These phrases are then "winnowed" to generate a set of 50 to 150 unique needs. The "winnowing" process eliminates duplicates and results in each need statement taking an affirmative form, preserving as much of the customer language as possible. The affirmative description of a pain or a need means that the set of statements will describe the ideal product or service, something to aspire to be. The phrases are then printed on small cards, one need statement per card.

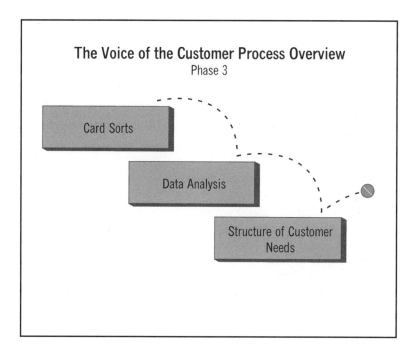

The Voice of the Customer Process Overview
Phase 3

Card Sorts

Data Analysis

Structure of Customer Needs

For Phase 3 of the Pain of the Customer Process, customers are recruited to sort the cards (attribute statements) into categories. The instructions are very simple: Put things together that go together in the mind of the customer. Card sorts can be done individually or in focus groups.

The analysis of the card sorts results in a hierarchy of customer needs being developed, containing three or more levels of detail, with the Pain of the Customer being expressed by the customer, in the customer's language, and as organized by the customer (i.e., the customers create the categories). The customers in the card-sort focus group can contribute a preliminary prioritization of the attribute list as well.

This hierarchy of needs can then be used to generate predictive internal measures (through Quality Function Deployment) and a quantitative survey for further analyses in the House of Quality or other techniques.

The structure of the hierarchy of needs can reveal as much as the individual attributes themselves. The way the customer organizes the needs can sometimes cross company boundaries or silos. For example, when calling your local utility because of a problem, the person you call is not the same person who comes to your house to fix the problem. We have seen occasions where these two utility employees report to different organizations all the way up to the vice-presidential level—one is in the call-center service organization, the other reports to the maintenance/field service organization. To the customer, the call for service is all one event.

If the call-center representative does a good job of taking the customer's concern into the company and sharing it with the field personnel, how would the customer know that? Suppose the field person shows up at the customer's home and says, "How can I help you?" The customer immediately thinks, "You mean you don't know?! I poured out my soul to the phone representative and none of that information was shared with you!" This customer may have experienced pain in the past from having an unprepared repair person arrive at her door.

Now, suppose that the field person said, "I see you have called about flickering lights. Can you show me the problem?" The field person is afraid that he may be wrong. He might look embarrassed to the customer and yet he almost always has this information available. If the information is correct, the customer's anxiety is greatly reduced. She thinks, "He knows why he is here. He knows what to do." Who gets the credit? The PHONE REP! The information was shared. If the information turns out to be incorrect, then the field person can continue with, "How can I help you?" He has lost nothing. The research has shown that one of the most important contributors to the phone representative's score on a customer-satisfaction survey is the way the field employee introduces himself.

Within the company, these two employees may be part of two different organizations. To the customer, they are two parts of the same transaction! This illustrates the fact that the customer's thoughts (wants, needs, and pains) are organized and the way the *company* is organized are sometimes very different.

As another example, consider the Silicon Valley company whose customers called customer service for severe problems, only to be greeted by an entitlement process that significantly delayed their problem being addressed. The employees engaged in the entitlement process did not report to the vice president in charge of customer service, so they were not measured in a way that encouraged speedy access to the service engineers. Obviously, the company and the customer had different metrics of success.

A Checklist of Lessons Learned

1. There is a step-by-step tried-and-tested way to gather and organize the Pain of the Customer, typically using one-on-one interviews.

2. Make sure you have done your homework before you begin interviewing customers.

3. The Pain of the Customer should describe the ideal product or service; the attributes should affirm that product or service (translate pains into affirmative statements).

4. Organize the need statements into categories as defined by customers, the way that they think of them. This structure can be very revealing and forms the basis for deriving a customer-satisfaction survey and predictive internal metrics.

5. The Pain of Customer and its structure can highlight issues of organizational structure or conflict.

9 Use the Pain of the Customer to Write Value Propositions

When Yogi Berra was once asked at spring training what size hat he wanted, he replied, "I don't know, I'm not in shape yet."[1]

Is your business 'in shape?' Do you know what you have to offer?

What is a "Value Proposition"?

The value proposition for your company or business is the statement of why your customers should give you money – what do they get in exchange for the money that they pay you?

How Do You Write One?

One of the toughest yet most important tasks that any business has to undertake is to explain to its customers why they should pay for the company's products and services. Why should they (your customers and consumers) give you money? What is the *value proposition*?

If you are a consultant flying on an airline, you are often asked by fellow passengers: "What services do you provide?" followed immediately by "That sounds interesting, who are your customers for that service, and why do they need a consultant for that?" In other words, "What is your value proposition?"

Customers make decisions based upon the value of the deal, not the price. After all, if price was the only factor in decision-making, wouldn't we all be traveling across the country on a Greyhound bus? We aren't. Why? Because we make such decisions based upon the utility of what we receive as compared to the price we pay, i.e., the value of the deal, where price has several attributes. The price attributes can range from initial cost to the hassle of dealing with you as a supplier to the long-term costs and many other cost-related factors.

Dr. Gale's book[2] addresses several issues: What is customer value and how is it managed? Who "owns" it? What are the specialized tools that are used to manage it? What data is needed? The market-research elements that Dr. Gale discusses include the "Pain of the Customer," customer-satisfaction survey data, and the "House of Quality."

A value proposition captures the essence of these ideas: What is the utility you receive from our products and services versus what does it cost you? Of course, the better the utilities are described by the marketer or salesperson, the better the perceived value by the customer. This is where the "Pain of the Customer" fits in. Marketing professionals have known for decades that customers respond best to ads that speak to their pain, both the fact that you understand it and the fact that you can solve it. Businesses behave the same way, especially with respect to "high-tech" products and services. They want their risk of pain alleviated.

Thus, for your value proposition to work, the customer must perceive that his pain or risk of pain will be reduced, or that there is an excitement about the positive attributes (features) of your product or service with minimal risk (pain avoidance).

5 Keys to a Great Value Proposition

1. Be able to express the value of your product or service in terms of how it solves or deals with the customer's pain, or how the customer benefits with minimized risk of pain.

2. Make sure you understand how much that pain costs them in terms of dollars, staff, time, hassle, and energy, i.e., the total cost.

3. Be sure to understand the costs of your product and service, both initially and long-term, including the hassles for the customer, if any.

4. Make sure you can articulate the value (the return) on the investment with your company in dollars and cents, and when payback should be expected. This necessarily involves analysis of the dollar value of benefits that may not be easily quantified.

5. Be aware of their alternatives (competitors to you or the option of doing nothing) and what advantages you have over each alternative;

proper value proposition analysis includes head-to-head comparisons with all of the customer's choices.

Be sure to expound on your Value Proposition on your Web site (see Chapter 28).

A Checklist of Lessons Learned

1. The Pain of Customer and its structure can help you to create a value proposition for your customers and segments of customers.

2. Understand your competition and your customer's perception of costs in order to write the best value proposition.

10 How to Manage Consultants the Pain-Point Way

A friend of co-author Chris Stiehl once suggested, "Why don't you become a consultant so you can insult people with impunity!"

There are many published articles concerning how to get the most out of a consulting relationship *if you are the customer[1]*. We have compiled a list of factors that your customers may value, shown below. These attributes are associated with them trying to avoid pain in their consulting relationship with you, whether you are the internal guru or the "hired gun."

All of us need to engage a specialist—a pro—to help us from time to time, but how do you make sure you get the most benefit for the money invested? A good general rule is that a consultant should generate several times your dollar investment in value returned.

We have recently had several conversations with some of our customers on this topic, as a way of continuously improving our services. We have conducted proprietary research and literature searches on the topic. Based upon those talks and published data, here are some important tips to remember:

1. **A Clear Reason for Hiring Them:** goals drive design. Why are you hiring this person? What skills do they have that you lack? What is the project's clearly defined objective? If the final report were available right now, what would be inside it? What would you be willing to do with that information? This upfront analysis can save money in the long run.

2. **Get the Right Expert:** seek referrals from friends and colleagues, and make sure they have the experience and skills you need. Avoid those who are just consulting between full-time jobs or as a part-time job.

3. **Check References:** be sure to ask how easy they are to work with; did they stay within budget, both on the work and the travel expenses? Would the reference use them again? Would they recommend them to a friend or colleague? What are their credentials in the area of your study? How many similar studies have they completed? How long ago?

4. **Establish Work Expectations:** have a timeline for deliverables. Make sure the consultant knows what dates are "hard" dates and which are softer; what data or information is "out of scope?" Make sure they have access to everything that they need. Be sure to ask for periodic reports of progress and difficulties. It is not uncommon to expect some "extra" contributions beyond the published Statement of Work. Make sure these are noted as they occur.

5. **Assess Your Organization's Readiness to Listen to the Consultant:** if the consultant is being hired to make recommendations, your organization needs to be ready to listen and act on them. Otherwise, the money you have spent is wasted. How ready are you? How ready is your management to act? What will be needed in terms of documentation to win the political battle as well as the logical battle (i.e., how will you answer the question, "You didn't speak to any of *my* customers?")? As stated previously (see #1 above), if the final report were completed already, what would it have in it and what would you do? You should know this answer before you begin!

6. **Make Sure Your Consultant is Paid on Time:** nothing can create problems with a project as quickly as unexpected or unexplained delays in travel reimbursement or payment for services. Make sure your company's payment policies are clear and up front to the consultant.

How does this list help you, the consultant, or individual contributor? We suggest that you use this as a list of potential pain points in a consulting relationship to be avoided. Make sure that your engagements have clear answers to all of these questions. This will result in a better likelihood of success for both you and your customer/client!

A Checklist of Lessons Learned

1. There are six key factors in having a successful engagement with a consultant.

11 The $3 Million Leather Seat

As Yogi Berra once said, "You can observe a lot just by watching!"[1]

What Does "Perfection" Mean?

A key lesson we have learned in our experience studying customers is to never assume you know what they want, or what they dislike (their "pain"); you must ask them! This is particularly true when defining "perfection." Often, the customers' view of perfection is different from the company view.

There once was a high school girl in San Diego who won several beauty titles and eventually competed in the Miss America contest. She was the "perfect" girl, right? A high school boy who often carpooled with her to school asked her who had invited her to the senior prom. "No one," she replied. "I had to ask a boy from another school because no one at our school would ask me!" Her classmates were too intimidated by "the perfect girl." They felt she was unapproachable. Someone may have asked her if she weren't so "perfect." Those who never thought to ask her missed out. So, what does this have to do with business and the pain of the customer?

The Perfect Leather Seat

In the late 1980s, Cadillac had what we thought was "perfect" leather. There were few, if any, belly wrinkles visible in leather seats in Cadillacs. There were no fly bites (resulting in small pinholes in the leather). Hides used by Cadillac had no mange or other clearly visible defect. The hides that were used came from cows that had not bumped into fences and allowed themselves to be scratched or scarred. If you visited a tanning facility, the hides that were acceptable to Cadillac were few in number, especially when compared to the leather that was used by other automotive manufacturers. Cadillac paid a premium for this "perfect," or near perfect, leather.

In order to make the leather durable in the Cadillac cars, a plastic-like coating was applied. Thus, you can imagine our surprise when Cadillac customers were surveyed and they expressed less than perfect satisfaction with the leather! In internal and external research the results were that Cadillac leather was not graded as highly as we had hoped (the data were similar to what is shown below). The customers thought they were being duped. This was not real leather. Surely, real leather would have more of what we at GM were calling defects (visible wrinkles and scratches).

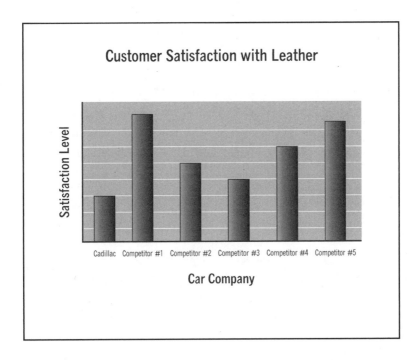

A market researcher responsible for understanding customer data, whether from GM's own studies or from J. D. Power studies, was given the job of trying to explain why Cadillac customers were not as happy with its leather as its competitors' customers were with their leather. He decided to execute a

"Pain of the Customer" study, including benchmarking Cadillac competitors.

As part of preparing to apply for the Malcolm Baldrige National Quality Award, Cadillac had studied the benchmarking techniques developed by Bob Camp and others at Xerox. Cadillac had also studied and implemented Quality Function Deployment (the "House of Quality"), or QFD, since 1982. Thus, Cadillac was prepared to execute a study of the depth that was needed.

Cadillac began by interviewing experts in the leather industry concerning what they felt customers valued in leather. The automaker spoke with people who manufactured shoes, briefcases, furniture, and athletic balls (footballs and basketballs). The market researcher learned a lot about leather, including where it comes from and how it is prepared for use in products. Cadillac was told that when people spend extra money for genuine-leather products, they want to be sure they have purchased real leather. The customer has fear (and potential pain) associated with being fooled; that is, thinking he had real leather when, in fact, he had synthetic material. In basketballs and footballs, for example, some "defects" were actually rolled into the leather mechanically! This was a far cry from the specifications set at Cadillac. The "defects" were called "natural markings" by the manufacturer. They contributed to the customer knowing that the leather was real.

Anyone who has ever purchased a new baseball glove knows the importance of the smell of the tanning agents and the suppleness of the leather when the glove comes out of its box. The leather experts also confirmed this for Cadillac: The smell of the leather and its suppleness are critical to customer satisfaction. These characteristics lead not only to the customer believing the leather is real, but also to the strong favorable memories and sensations of leather—the "richness." These emotions have been known to be triggered by aromas. This was obviously a desirable quality for Cadillacs!

Interviewing leather experts in various non-competing industries helped Cadillac develop an interview guide for speaking with luxury-automotive customers, both Cadillac customers and competitors' customers. None of the industries that were polled in the benchmarking were direct competitors to Cadillac, so the experts spoke freely.

Next, the market researcher spoke with internal experts, including some of the same people who had defined Cadillac specifications, to gain their perspective. A few of the people who had been hired into Cadillac had worked for other luxury-car manufacturers. The market researcher sought out these people. One told the researcher that one competitor actually sprayed a scent into their cars before giving them back to the customers after servicing. The scent was designed to mimic the smell of tanning agents.

Another transplant from a competitor said that at a dealership where he had worked, a powder was spread on the front seat track to give off an aroma of the tanning agents when the front seat was moved. Again, what did they know that Cadillac did not?

Letting the Customer Define Defects

Only then, after thorough benchmarking, did the Cadillac market researcher start observing and interviewing luxury-car owners. First, customers use their hands, noses, and eyes to evaluate leather. Observing their behavior as they interacted with the seats told the researcher most of what he needed to know about what the customers were looking for. They run their hands across the material to feel the suppleness. They want to smell the tanning agents, the aroma. They also look for a few subtle reminders that the leather is natural, so-called natural markings (what Cadillac had called *defects!*). When they were interviewed, customers spoke about the appearance, feel, and smell of leather. In the case of Cadillac, the coating that was designed to provide durability eliminated the suppleness and smell of the leather. With no "natural markings," customers thought the leather was too perfect. In other words, fake. They thought it might be artificial, as there were no wrinkles, scratches, or other markings that natural leather had. When the researcher asked what the owners wanted, they told him that the smell and feel were important, and there should be a few natural markings to prove it was real leather, but not too many. Obviously, a large scar or scratch in a highly visible location was undesirable. However, a small scratch or wrinkle was not a problem.

Cadillac then had seats fabricated with varying levels of natural markings in various locations on the seats. The market researcher then asked luxury customers and prospective luxury owners to evaluate the seats and describe their likes and dislikes. Thus, Cadillac was able to develop standards for natural markings at various locations in the seat. The standards varied considerably from the seat pan, to the back and sides, based upon how visible the area was. The new standards were very different from the "zero tolerance" standards Cadillac had previously employed. Cadillac standards were now based upon the likes and dislikes of the customers, and the pain they had experienced or feared they might experience if the leather turned out not to be real.

Going One Step Further: Eliciting an Emotional Response

The research and development department was busy developing a new coating. Their goal was to reintroduce suppleness and aroma into Cadillac leather while not backing off on the durability needs of the customers. Several scents that were developed were tested in order to find the one that reminded customers the most of the smell of leather. The coating that was developed allowed for a suppler feel while releasing a mild aroma of tanning agents, particularly when exposed to sunlight. The smell and feel of the leather seats were designed to elicit a strong emotional response of luxury. Observing the customers interacting with the car, as mentioned before, strongly indicated that we had been successful: The customers smiled and made exciting comments when looking at the leather, smelling it, and feeling it.

The new leather specifications were implemented in the early 1990s by Cadillac, and were offered to the other marketing divisions of General Motors at the same time. The customer satisfaction with Cadillac's leather increased, while the cost of the leather decreased dramatically. Estimates in the early 1990s were that approximately $25,000 had been spent "out of pocket" on research (clinics and other customer-interface activities). The estimated cost savings were up to several million dollars per year company-wide! Thus, the Pain of the Customer and benchmarking research had a significant return on investment.

How to Apply This Story to Your Business

Of course, over time, standards change and customer opinions change. The result of this research, however, was a dramatically increased perception of what was and was not important to Cadillac customers. The automaker then stressed the factors that elicited the strongest emotional response of luxury to its customers. Cadillac had a dramatically new and different set of leather specifications. Some of the things Cadillac learned were apparently already known to its competitors. The question is: What do your competitors know about your customers and their pains and preferences that you don't know?

If you exceed the performance being requested by your customers, make sure they value the performance you have achieved. Polaroid once specified a level of defects it was willing to tolerate in some parts it was having fabricated by a supplier. The supplier sent Polaroid the order, with the defective parts in a baggy on the top of thousands of beautiful parts. They'd already sorted them out and had enclosed a note stating, "We don't know why you wanted this level of defects, but they are enclosed in the baggy. The rest are good!" Polaroid got what it had asked for. The supplier had met Polaroid specifications, including the level of defects, literally!

No one tries to have defects, but make sure your attempts to eliminate them are truly what the customers want, expect, and are willing to pay for.

The reader may want to refer back to the Customer-Driven Improvement Model in Chapter 3 to note how this example follows that pattern: incorporating the Pain of the Customer (customer pains with our previous leather design), good internal metrics (and the research needed to determine what a good score would be), external surveys (which prompted the project), and steps to improve (including extensive Benchmarking).

Consider the previously-mentioned story of a Silicon Valley company and the call-in process for customer service. In this instance, the company knows that it has a problem or the customer would not be calling. Yet, they have deliberately instituted a delay in service in order to make sure that the customer is entitled to service on the device that has failed. In this case, prior to the transfer of the call to the service engineer, the metric of success for the company is the reduction of costs associated with repairing devices that are not under a service contract. The metric of success for the customer is to reduce the time required to restore service. The overall definition of success for the company for the call is to restore service quickly. Yet their metric for the entitlement portion has nothing to do with speed. This conflict could only be resolved by a complete analysis through the Customer-Driven Improvement Model. The result was to change the organizational structure to have the entitlement process mirror the customers' need for speedy service.

A Checklist of Lessons Learned

1. Let the customer describe "perfection" and "defects" in their own terms; don't assume you know what they want or what they fear (their potential pain). Make sure you ask!

2. Ask yourself who else is dealing with issues like yours in a non-competitive industry; you can benchmark them to gain clues as to how to solve your issues. Be observant of how the issues are dealt with by others.

3. Talk to former employees and customers of competitors, if you can find them, to learn how they dealt with the problems.

4. Invest in market research to develop the right specifications; test them with customers. Getting the correct emotional response to your product can result in a tremendous financial benefit.

5. After you have met the customers' needs, double check with them that you have truly understood what they were looking for and what they were afraid might happen to them, their potential pain.

12 Changing Needs Over Time: The Kano Model

"Nothing is constant but change"[1]

Don't Needs Change Over Time?

Every element of your business feels that their customer needs are "unique." Every member of your sales and marketing staff typically feels that needs are constantly changing. In our experience, it is rare that needs change. Usually, it is the priorities of the needs that change from time to time or from one segment to another.

If you worked for General Motors, you would find research on customer wants, needs, and pains dating back to the early 1920s in the research library. The needs would look eerily similar to those of GM's customers today. For example, if you looked at the pictures of Will Durant and Henry Ford sitting in an open-cabin automobile early in the twentieth century, you would see they were dressed in warm coats and hats, inside the car. Obviously, people have wanted to be comfortable in a car for decades—that need has not changed. What has changed is the priority of that need. By the 1920s, cars had closed cabins and the automotive manufacturers began offering a heater inside the car as an option. By the 1940s and 1950s, who would buy a car without a heater? Meeting this need was no longer an option, but a necessity. Air conditioners were an option in the early 1990s. Now, the automotive manufacturers offer individual front- and rear-seat "climate zones," each with their own controls. Has the need changed? No, but the solutions and the priority placed on meeting that need by the customer and the car manufacturer have changed over time.

Cadillac executed Pain of the Customer studies for one of the Cadillac models ten years apart. Less than 10% of the needs changed, even though the solutions as implemented in the car were dramatically different. The same truth applies to other industries. In a similar study for medical devices, the doctors, nurses, and patients had very different priorities, but over 90% of their needs were the same.

Of course, at times, needs *do* change. In our experience, the Pain of the Customer should be revisited about once every four or five years to look for "new" needs. Priorities should be examined more often by surveying customers concerning the importance of each need (more on this in the next chapter).

The Kano Model

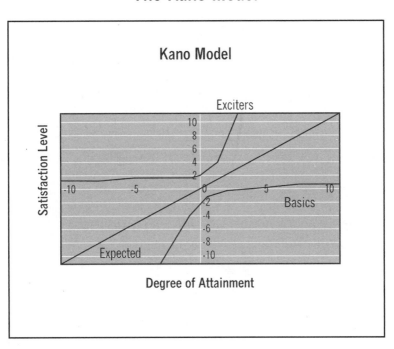

The Kano Model[2] describes the types of needs that customers have as well as the types of metrics and solutions that companies implement. Meeting some needs is a cost of entry into a market. These needs do not contribute appreciably to customer satisfaction, but not meeting them can create significant dissatisfaction. This is shown graphically above. The better job a product or service does at meeting a basic need, the closer it is to zero on the customer-satisfaction scale.

Meeting some needs results in incremental improvements in customer satisfaction, while not meeting them results in incremental customer-satisfaction penalties. The satisfaction of these needs is expected. These are the standard features of your product or service that many of your competitors have that satisfy needs.

There are some needs that are "exciters." Meeting these needs is a big plus, while not meeting them does not result in a penalty. These are the "silver bullets" that top management is often seeking in new product developments.

Most needs go through each of these phases in their lifetime, starting as an "exciter" and progressing through "expected" to becoming a "basic." A key factor in meeting a need is understanding the type of need you are considering. Recall the story mentioned previously of the pictures of Henry Ford and Will Durant in hats and overcoats. They had a need for comfort in their automobile, but this was difficult to achieve in an open cab. A heater was impractical. Over the next several decades, this need went from being an exciter in the 1920s, to an expected feature in the 1940s, to a basic feature - no one would by a car without a heater today.

Car companies are attempting to make this need an exciter again by creating "individual climate zones," both front and rear.

A Checklist of Lessons Learned

1. The Kano Model describes the different types of needs and the natural progression of a need through different stages of development.

13 How Do I Develop Good Internal Predictive Metrics?

Have you ever thought..."I am drowning in data, but I'm dying for some information!"?

Translating Data Into Information

The discussion of the Customer-Driven Improvement Model presented earlier was an attempt to convince you that at least some of your company metrics should be predictive of success with your customers. Companies have tons of data and reports, but little information. Companies appear to be especially poor in internal predictive metrics. As mentioned previously, customer-satisfaction data, while informative, is like driving down the road looking in the rearview mirror. It tells you what happened in the past, not how customers will feel in the future. Consider the fresh-popcorn example. The movie-theater owner does not need to survey moviegoers about the popcorn. He knows it is only a few minutes old; therefore, he knows it is fresh.

Make Sure You Don't Pick Just Any Customer Metrics, Pick GOOD Ones!

Are you struggling to understand what is truly important to your customers? Do you have GOOD internal metrics, that is, metrics that can predict success with the customers? Most companies have many metrics and a lot of data, but few GOOD ones and often without much information. How do you decide what a good metric is? The best internal metrics have several key characteristics:

The Seven Keys to Having GOOD Customer Metrics on Your Dashboard

1. They are predictive of success with customers. (Note: They are linked to customer needs and they look forward in time, not backward like surveys.)

2. They are measurable. (You can specify how to generate a number.)

3. They are controllable. (You can take actions that change the value of the metric.)

4. The desired value(s) can be specified. (You know what a good score is.)

5. The interaction with other metrics is known. (If action is taken to change this metric, the effect on other metrics is known.)

6. The metric is repeatable, i.e., if the metric is taken twice, you are likely to get the same value.

7. The metric is easily implemented.

Of course, few metrics survive this gauntlet. In our experience, the first criterion eliminates the most metrics from surviving the list. Many reports and much of the data that is collected in companies are designed to measure things that do not impact customers directly.

How do we know if the metric is linked to a customer need, want, or pain? One test for this characteristic is to track the metric and the related customer-satisfaction data. If you execute an improvement initiative and it has a measurable impact on the internal metric (as described in the Customer-Driven Improvement Model), there should be a corresponding change in the customer-satisfaction data. If this does not occur, then either your metric is not predictive, or you have not changed the internal metric in a range of values corresponding to the sensitivities of the customer (discussed in the next chapter). The relationship between the customer-satisfaction data and the internal metric is a very important graph to obtain. This is not easily done and it takes time, but this allows you to set standards for the internal metric and identify benchmarking opportunities.

How do we know if the metric is measurable? This requires that you can specify the way that a number is obtained. Many things that people typically think are not measurable may be converted to a number in some way. For instance, would you have predicted you could measure how fresh popcorn tastes? The key is to not look for necessarily a precise metric, but one that does an adequate job of differentiating different levels of performance on the issue at hand. The tough part of this criterion is the specificity that is required. Where does the data come from? Who obtains it? What is done with it to create the metric?

What does controllable mean? This is a criterion that often results in a "maybe" or "partial" response from our customers. The point is that you can take action inside the company to cause the number to change in a predictable way. For example, can you control the weather? In most business settings, temperature, lighting, and humidity may be controlled. Isn't that controlling the weather?

You may have to benchmark others to know what a good score is, but that knowledge is important. We have already mentioned the possibility of having a score that is in a range of relative insensitivity to the customer. This is one of the reasons you need to know what a good score is. In a later chapter on benchmarking, we will discuss making sure you have thought through who else might use a metric like yours, perhaps from a noncompetitive industry. They may be able to give you a benchmark target score.

Interactions between metrics are common, but are often not documented. If you improve one metric through an improvement initiative, you should be aware of what other metrics are impacted and how. The House of Quality (discussed in a later chapter) illustrates the importance of this knowledge and how to mitigate the negative impacts.

The metric should be repeatable. In some cases, taking the measurement can influence the outcome. The best metrics can be repeated with results or outcomes that do not change significantly.

If a metric is easy to implement, that is desirable as well. Some metrics need to be altered to fit these criteria, and that may cost time, effort, or money. Obviously, it is not desirable for the expense of executing the metric to outweigh the benefits.

The best metrics combine quantity and quality into one metric. Consider the call-volume metric we have already discussed. If we simply measure the number of calls handled by a telephone representative, we might encourage behavior that is undesirable: rushing the customer, not completely satisfying the customer, or worse. In one call center we actually witnessed a telephone rep deliberately using his telephone plug to "answer" a dozen calls in thirty seconds. By this metric (call volume), he would get a good score! Now, consider the first call satisfaction metric. This metric combines quality (customer is satisfied) and quantity (how quickly this can be accomplished). This metric encourages the employee to develop skills to satisfy the customer completely, and continuously improve how quickly this can be done. When we have seen this metric implemented properly, both customers and employees were more satisfied.

This discussion points to the need to develop metrics that are not easily "gamed" by the employees. At least, if they are gamed, the behavior exhibited by the employees results in customer needs being met.

What is the Health of Your Metrics?

Check the health of your internal metrics and make sure they lead to the results (behavior, internal data and customer satisfaction data) you desire. It takes a disciplined approach to make sure the "pain" of your customers is deployed properly in your organization's customer relationships and reflected in your key metrics.

Having good predictive metrics enables you to anticipate customer needs and, in some cases, meet their needs before they have been articulated to you!

BIZARRO/By Piraro

In our view, this cartoon represents the perfect business model. The owner of Psychic Pizza knows and understands his customers so well that he can anticipate their needs.

A Checklist of Lessons Learned

1. There is a step-by-step way to evaluate internal metrics and decide if they are "GOOD" customer-oriented metrics.

2. The best metrics meet seven criteria that would allow company data to be translated into information.

3. The best metrics combine quantity and quality into one metric.

14 How Do I Test My Metrics?

"A fortune cookie or an astrologer are bound to be right some of the time."[1]

What Happens If My Metric Does Not Predict Well?

There are two basic checks of a predictive internal metric. First, if your predictive internal metric suggests that the customer-satisfaction data should change (either up or down) and if the change does not happen, then you may not have a good predictor. In our experience this usually indicates that there are some elements of what the customer is thinking about that are not captured in your predictive internal metric.

The Fisher Body Division of General Motors provides a good example of where the metric was not as predictive as the company had hoped. One of the questions on the customer-satisfaction survey (and one of the customer needs/pains) dealt with door-closing effort. The customers wanted the doors to close securely with minimal effort on their part. GM measured a number of cars in the marketplace and plotted their customer satisfaction versus the measured effort in foot-pounds required to close the door from a full open position. While there was a general trend toward a higher satisfaction score at lower efforts, there was a lot of scatter in the data. There were some car models that had similar measured efforts while having significantly different satisfaction scores. The best-fitting curve to the data was informative, but not completely predictive.

GM went back to the customers to discuss what they were thinking about when they answered that question on the survey. Surely, they were thinking about the physical effort involved, but other factors as well. They thought about how the door felt on its hinges. They thought about the sound the door made as it swung closed, and the sound it made at closing (did it sound hollow or tinny, or did it sound solid?). The effort and comfort of the door handle were factors as well. Thus, the effort to close the door was important, but that alone did not capture all nuances of "door-closing effort." Another issue was: Did the question refer to effort from inside or outside the car? They had assumed it was from outside, but not all customers thought this way.

Secondly, the metric may do a good job of predicting the customers' votes on a customer-satisfaction survey, but you may currently be in a range of the relationship where your improvements are not noticed.

Again, considering door-closing effort, the sensitivity curve below illustrates the relationship between customer satisfaction and the foot-pounds required to close the door. At the time, GM was so low on the performance scale (high effort) that when the automaker cut the effort in half to close the car door, it was still at twice the effort of GM competitors! When GM made the improvements, the customers did not notice; the door was still much too difficult to close.

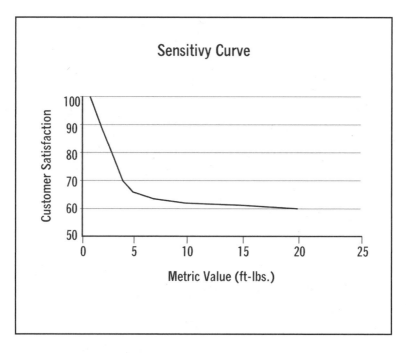

Once the door-closing effort entered a range where the customers were able to notice the change, the data in the surveys changed as GM made improvements.

As market researchers were studying this issue at Fisher Body, they faced a dilemma. In order to prevent water leaks and wind noise, GM needed to have tight seals on the doors. If GM had tight seals, there was nowhere for the air to escape as the door was closing, so door closing effort increased. In GM's analysis for the door of a car, these two metrics interacted negatively (shared a negative sign in the "roof" of the House of Quality—see Chapter 15). The solution? The air needed a way to escape while we maintained a low probability of wind noise or water leaks. GM decided to cut a hole in the rear seat so the air would be able to escape into the trunk. Thus, the pass-through rear seat was developed. The marketing staff found that this feature could be sold to customers as a benefit, e.g. being able to haul skis in a sedan and get into the trunk from the rear seat. This demonstrates how conflicts between metrics (as shown in the roof of the House of Quality) can result in innovation and creativity.

A Checklist of Lessons Learned

1. For any of your important internal predictive metrics, develop the sensitivity curve to establish where you are on the curve and to define targets for technical performance. (For example, what goal for effort would you set if you wanted 95% customer satisfaction?)

2. There are two tests for metrics to make sure they are accomplishing the predictive power that you desire.

3. Conflicts between metrics can lead to innovation.

15 The House of Quality (Quality Function Deployment)

W. E. Deming once said, "In God we trust. All others must use data!"[1]

What is the House of Quality?

The House of Quality is a document and a process that connects the key business metrics and strategies to the Pain of the Customer. We will not discuss the details of how to build a House of Quality in this chapter. However, we will present information to convince you that this methodology is worth learning. The earlier "bubble diagram" (the Customer-Driven Improvement Model) illustrating the need to connect the customer wants, needs, and pains to predictive internal metrics, customer-satisfaction surveys, and improvement initiatives was an abbreviated diagram of a House of Quality.

The main idea behind the House of Quality is to make choices. Who among us has infinite time, staff, or money? No one does! Thus, you must make choices about how and where to invest time, staff, and money. The House of Quality enables you to choose among options and to select the options that generate the "biggest bang for the buck" invested. The House helps you maximize the impact on customer satisfaction of the improvement initiatives you can afford to select. The House will also enable you to predict changes in customer-satisfaction scores as a result of your initiatives, both positive and negative changes. It will provide you with areas for research and development (interactions between metrics) and for benchmarking (the "winning" metrics).

The House of Quality was developed in Japan in the early 1970s[2] and brought to the United States in the early 1980s by the automotive industry. For example, General Motors worked on its first House of Quality in 1982. U.S. companies, beginning with the "big three" in Detroit, have adapted the House of Quality successfully into their business culture. As you can see below, the House looks complicated. Please remember that it is as simple as the "bubble diagram" discussed previously.

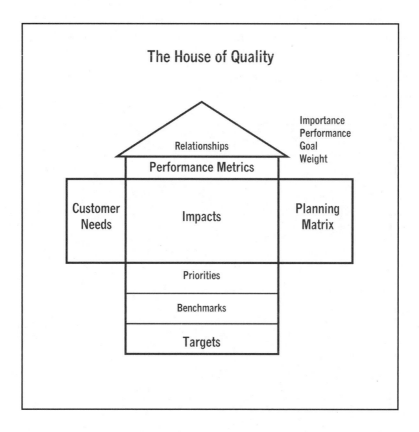

Can you see how this diagram mimics the Customer-Driven Improvement Model from Chapter 4? Rotate the diagram above 90 degrees to the right, and they are identical.

The Balloon Factory Example

This example was inspired by a colleague attempting to describe the House of Quality process. Let's assume that you manufacture balloons for the county fair. You have a competitor who also sells balloons to the kids at the fair. The "pain" is pretty simple: Kids want balloons that are BIG and BLUE, and that FLOAT. These would be entered as "customer needs."

What metrics would predict success with these needs? The amount of gas in the balloon would predict the size of the balloon and how much it floats. The thickness of the plastic would predict how big the balloon could get and how transparent it would become (lack of blueness). The amount of pigment in the plastic would also predict how blue the balloon was. These would be entered as "performance metrics."

1	2	3	4	5	6	7	8	9	10
	Amount of Gas in the Balloons	Thickness of the Plastic	Amount of Pigment in the Plastic	Importance to the Kids	Performance of My Balloons in Surveys	Competitor's Score	Goal in Survey	Ratio	Weight
BIG	9	3	0	5	4	5	5	1.25	6.25
BLUE	-1	3	9	3	5	3	4	0.80	2.40
FLOATS	9	1	0	4	4	4	5	1.25	5.00
STRENGTH OF THE METRIC	98.85	30.95	21.60						

The rest of the House of Quality is built with survey data and management goals (the "planning matrix"), analysis of the metrics ("relationships" and "impacts"), and benchmarking metrics (setting technical goals). The relationships between the metrics and the "pain" are described by their strength ("impacts"). These strengths are weighted (9, 3, 1, or 0). A team of employees representing multiple functions within the organization develops the list of internal predictive metrics and evaluates their strength in predicting success with the customer needs. The same team evaluates the metrics to determine if they interact with each other, either negatively (improving one metric actually hurts another) or synergistically (improving one metric also improves another).

As shown in the table above, survey data from the customers (kids at the fair, in this case) about your balloons and your competitor's balloons are a key part of the analysis (columns 6 and 7). The importance scores from the same survey for each need are entered in column 5. The management or the House of Quality team sets the goals for the future product in column 8. The ratio of column 8 to column 6 indicates how much improvement is needed to achieve the goal. This is shown in column 9. This ratio is multiplied by the importance score from column 5 to generate a set of weights for the needs. The most important element of this calculation is that the current customer-satisfaction score, management's goals, and the importance of the needs to the customer are captured in one weight. What about the other entries in the matrix?

Columns 2, 3, and 4 are created by the House of Quality team. Each internal predictive metric is judged as to how well it predicts success with each need, with, by convention, a "9" being the sign of strong ability to predict success with customers, a "3" being moderate, a "1" being weak predictive power, and a "0" being the sign that the metric is not related to the need. The "-1" in column 2 indicates that putting more gas within the balloon reduces the blueness, as the balloon expands and the plastic stretches. This convention grants the greatest weight to metrics that predict strongly.

The metrics are evaluated by multiplying the weight of each need by the entries in columns 2, 3, and 4 and then adding in columns. Thus, the amount of gas in the balloon is by far the strongest metric in achieving our goals with customers.

The point here is not to articulate how the calculations are done, but rather, to illustrate how the customer and company data combine to enable you to decide what metrics (and therefore what strategies) will have the greatest impact on the customer.

If you examine the first two metrics (columns 2 and 3), they interact. The thinner the plastic (to allow for the balloon to be bigger and float better), the less gas would be allowed — too much gas and the balloon would burst. This information is what is captured in the "roof" — the "relationships" part of the House of Quality. Such interactions create opportunities for research to resolve the issue — a chance to create breakthroughs and innovation.

Additional technical information is captured in the bottom of the House — technical benchmarks for each metric (for you and your competitor) and targets for your product or service design. In the example above, we have set a goal of increasing the customer reaction to our balloons in terms of size and their ability to float. This means more gas should be used. On the other hand, we can afford to back off a little with respect to blueness. We are already ahead of our competitor significantly and it is not very important to the kids. Thus, we can set our target to have a little more gas in our balloons than the competitor, while reducing the amount of pigment in our plastic, still being bluer than our competitor. The strategy is to take the money we are saving on pigment and invest it in more gas—all based upon customer data and our benchmark analysis of the competition!

We are trying to influence the value perception from the big equation of business (Chapter 2) to create the customer's perception that our balloon is a better deal than that of the competition.

Once the initial House of Quality is built, additional Houses (matrices) can be built to study the impact of strategies or proposed improvement initiatives on the metrics and customer needs.

House of Quality Do's and Don'ts

There are a number of important things to remember when building a House of Quality, lessons learned from twenty-five years of using this process.

Do's" and "Don'ts"

1. DO make sure you have a Pain of the Customer (wants, needs, and pains) from an objective third party, in customer language, organized the way the customer thinks.

2. DO make sure all relevant segments are included in the "Pain."

3. DO design your customer satisfaction survey using the "Pain."

4. DO make sure that everyone who may be affected by the outcome of the Team has his or her interests represented somehow on the team.

5. DON'T have your team be more than is needed. Six to eight is good; ten is a lot; twelve is too many.

6. DON'T have too many "9s." Each 9 says you can strongly predict success with a customer need. No one is that good.

7. DON'T have every goal set at the highest mark; that's unrealistic.

8. DO design metrics that meet the key criteria:
   A. Relate to or predict meeting a need
   B. Are measurable (I can get a number.)
   C. Are controllable (I can make the number change.)
   D. Desired outcomes are known (I know what a good score is.)
   E. Interactions are known (I know how improving this metric affects others.)
   F. Are repeatable (If I measure twice, I'm likely to get the same number or close to it.)
   G. Hopefully, are easy to implement

9. DON'T make *quantitative* assumptions about *qualitative* data.

10. DO trust the process. It works!

11. DO complete the whole "House," including the roof, and build second and third "Houses" to analyze strategic plans and evaluate alternatives.

12. DON'T debate "1s" and "3s"—everyone does it and it is a waste of time.

13. DO have at least one "9" (or three "3s") for each category of need. DON'T have metrics with no "9s" if it can be avoided.

14. DO make the appropriate adjustments to the "House" based upon

survey data or evaluations of metrics (benchmarking, etc.).

Reaping the complete benefits of building the House of Quality takes place over several years. As we have illustrated in this book, building the Voice of the Customer and the House of Quality is a rigorous process. Our clients have seen significant benefits for this investment in product and service design, even given the short product life cycles prevalent in Silicon Valley (PDAs, routers, cell phones, medical devices, etc.).

A Checklist of Lessons Learned

1. The House of Quality is a rigorous process that leads to having the customer wants and needs leading the evaluation of potential improvement initiatives.

2. The House of Quality process requires a multifunctional team using a disciplined approach.

3. The House of Quality can illustrate the need for benchmarking, for research-and-development projects, and for reducing costs. If you have to make cuts, the House can tell you where they will have the least impact on the customer.

16 How Do I Develop Good Customer-Satisfaction Surveys?

In the movie *A Few Good Men*, Jack Nicholson's character is famous for saying "You can't handle the truth!"

Maybe for this chapter, it should be, "You can't afford the truth!"

Start with the Pain of the Customer

One of the biggest problems in survey work, whether done by mail, telephone, or online, is the response rate. Even the best of surveys typically have potentially large nonresponse biases. They are good and accurate indicators of change, but each methodology mentioned above has obvious reasons why certain segments of the population would not respond to them. For example, middle-aged men generally do not respond as easily to mail surveys, while senior citizens *do* typically respond better to mail surveys. However, the latter may not respond well to online surveys, while middle-aged men may respond better to that medium. Given the potential nonresponse issues in each methodology, the only way to obtain the "true scores" reliably would be to conduct a census. Who can afford to do that? For your biggest or best customers, that may be practical. For most businesses, conducting a census is impractical and expensive.

How can we increase response rates and decrease the potential for nonresponse bias? We need to ask questions that customers want to respond to, questions that they find meaningful. How are your questions developed now? Often they are developed by internal sources or an objective third party. This will work fairly well as long as people who interact with customers are represented in those processes. Sometimes focus groups are held to have customers describe what they think each question means to them. However, what if the customers wrote the questions?

We will show you an articulated Pain of the Customer. It is organized the way the customers thought about welfare-to-work programs offered by state and Federal agencies for youth. The example is for businesses that receive prospective youth employees from the agencies after receiving job training. Each category was developed by business customers to categorize the wants and needs of fellow business owners. There are four major categories (in italics) and nine secondary categories of needs (in bold). The rest of the needs are individual attribute statements that have been organized and prioritized by business owners (the customers).

Youth Employee Qualities

The Quality Of The Youth That The Agency Sends Us

The Youth have good attendance.

The Youth come to work on time every day.

I can contact parents and/or staff concerning attendance issues.

The Youth can spell, read, and do basic math.

Youth have the capacity to learn the job.

Youth have good work habits (no "bad" ones learned previously).

Youth have a commitment to the job, even if the job is short-term.

Youth have been taught what it takes to get along in life outside of school.

Youth Qualities Match The Job We Are Trying To Fill

Youth express a strong interest in the job (follow-up independently after the interview).

I have the appropriate number of Youth from which to choose.

Youth are well-prepared (dress, attitude, etc.) for a job interview.

Youth have transportation to and from the job.

Youth can work the hours we need.

Youth can work at the location(s) we need.

I can mold (train) the Youth to meet our needs.

Youth dress and behave appropriately.

Youth understand this is work and NOT school (there is a job to do).

The Youth really want to work here.

Agency Is Well-Run

Agency staff members are professional and ethical.

Agency staff members follow through on their tasks until completion.

Agency employees care about my needs as much as their own and those of the Youth.

Ensure that the time and effort I invest in working with the agency will pay off.

Agency staff members provide good customer service.

Staff members are responsive and reliable.

Return my phone calls promptly.

Treat my time as valuable.

Agency staff helps plan and mediate between us and the Youth.

Monitor the performance of the Youth and provide assistance we needed.

Evaluations (exit interviews) are taken seriously and benefit the Youth, employer, and agency. (Did everyone learn what they were supposed to learn?)

Agency staff members are competent; they know what they are doing.

The information I give the agency is properly processed.

I get consistent answers from staff members.

Staff listens to my needs and requirements with respect to the Youth they send for an interview.

Staff understands my business and what it takes for my business to succeed.

Staff lets me know what services are available to me as the employer of the Youth.

Support Services

Reasonable and workable internal procedures.

If the Youth is not working out, I can interview additional Youth for the job.

Contracting and reporting requirements are not a burden.

We receive our contracted payments (when required) on time.

Forms are easy to fill out and understand for Youth programs.

Training and educational opportunities.

Help me find ways to contribute to the development of Youth in the community.

Youth get involved in voluntary community activities through work.

Help me find ways to make our community grow and prosper.

They offer training seminars relevant to hiring Youth.

Help me network with other Youth employers.

Keep me informed of rules and regulations.

I receive up-to-date information on regulations relevant to hiring Youth and Workforce Investment Act programs.

Educate me about the tax advantages of the agency programs

Give me up-to-date information for the hiring process.

Let me know how to take advantage of your programs and services.

Keep me informed about any changes in the Youth programs.

Keep me up-to-date concerning interviewing do's and don'ts.

Tell me how Youth experiences with my business compare to other businesses that hire Youth.

The secondary level in the hierarchy of needs can be easily translated into survey questions. Doing so will ensure that the questions that are asked are important to customers and worded in their language. Many company surveys are written in "company speak" or use language that customers may not use. By writing the survey questions using the Pain of the Customer, you get a higher response rate and make sure the customers' issues are being addressed. In addition, when you get a low score on one of these questions, you have the detail from the individual attributes in the hierarchy to articulate what the customers were thinking about.

Your survey strategy should include asking about the importance of each attribute to your customers periodically and surveying the customers of your competitors. The competitor data is needed for the House of Quality (see Chapter 15) and for potentially segmenting your market. If your competitor's customers have different priorities than your customers, this can lead to marketing opportunities or product- and service-development opportunities for you. If they have different satisfaction scores, you may be able to generate competitor-specific sales strategies to make use of your product's advantages and minimize the exposure of your weaknesses. A good example of the use of the Pain of the Customer techniques in survey design was Cisco Systems being awarded the coveted J.D. Power and Associates certification for technology service and support excellence by the Service & Support Professionals Association (SSPA) and J.D. Power and Associates for the second consecutive year in 2006.

What is the Health of Your Customer-Satisfaction Surveys?

Check the health of your customer-satisfaction surveys and make sure they lead to the results you can interpret (i.e., results that are predicted by your internal metrics). There are two quick checks on the health of your surveys. First, use an "overall" question to perform regression analysis on the individual questions to make sure they do a good job of predicting the outcome. Your r^2 should indicate how well your survey questions reflect the overall experience of your customers. Questionnaires designed using the methodology described above often score higher on this criterion than surveys designed internally. Secondly, you should at least occasionally ask the customer to rate the importance of each question. These ratings will also indicate if the customers find one or more questions unimportant. The importance data, in our experience, do not change often, although they may vary considerably by segment. The importance data are significant for use in the House of Quality.

A Checklist of Lessons Learned

1. There is a step-by-step way to write "GOOD" customer-oriented customer-satisfaction surveys using the Pain of the Customer. (For example, have the customer essentially write the questions.)

2. The best survey questions use customer language, not "company speak," and they lead to reduced risk of nonresponse bias, i.e., they lead to higher response rates.

3. Surveys designed using the hierarchy of needs (the Pain) provide a means for interpreting the results (the detail in the hierarchy amplifies the responses).

4. There are two easy ways to check the health of your survey questions.

5. You should periodically ask importance questions and survey your competitors' customers.

17 Importance vs. Performance

"Eighty percent of American managers cannot answer
with any measure of confidence these seemingly simple questions: What is my job? What in it really counts?
How well am I doing?"[1]

How Do I Know What to Work On?

One of the lessons in the House of Quality is to learn to weigh the needs of the customer based upon your gaps in current performance, the importance of the needs to the customer, and your corporate goals. All three of these factors are present in the "Planning Matrix" in the House (see Chapter 15). Customers are surveyed on the importance of each need, as well as on how well those needs are being met. Management (or the House of Quality team) sets goals for customer satisfaction, based upon importance data, current performance, and data on competitors. Typically, the House of Quality uses all of this information. The ratio of the management goal for each need to the current actual performance can be used to indicate the percentage of improvement needed to obtain the goal. Multiplying this ratio by the customer importance score creates a new weighting for the needs. The new weighting incorporates all three elements: importance, performance, and management goals—into one score. Why did the Japanese do this?

They were attempting to create more weight for needs statements with high importance and low performance. These needs are the highest priority—those that will generate the greatest impact when they are met. These are the needs where you and your customers have the most to gain and are very important.

Of course, you have to measure importance to know this. In our experience, many companies measure customer satisfaction, but few measure the customers' perceptions of the importance of each pain or need. We recommend that a company performs this type of importance research every year or two to make sure that the customers' priorities have not changed.

In the diagram below, what we are seeking is the pains and needs (survey questions) that fall into the upper-left quadrant. What is shown is some sample data from a typical study. Both importance and performance were measured on a 1 to 5 scale. The scales are set to reflect the average scores on each scale at the origin. There are three survey questions that clearly fall into the targeted quadrant. These are the items where high impact can be realized if success can be obtained.

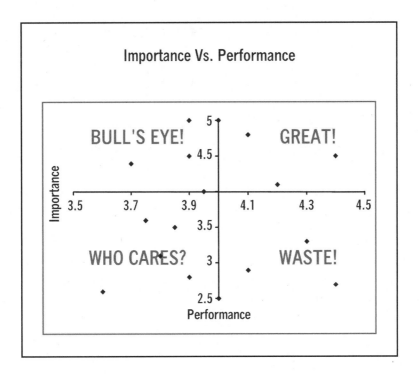

The upper-right quadrant is good news: items where importance matches performance in the high range of the scales. Items in the quadrant of low importance and low performance are items that should be monitored, but do not warrant investment in improvement initiatives at the moment. We have seen many companies who do not have importance data invest in all items where the customer-satisfaction score was low. As you can see above, some of these items are unimportant to the customer. However, if you do not measure importance, how would you know this? Whatever investments have lead to higher performance in some of the low-importance issues are wasted. The company is exceeding what is required or expected by the customer, but the customer does not care! A reduction in investments in this quadrant could lead to finances being available to invest in issues at the bull's-eye! This is a simplified version of what the Panning Matrix in the House of Quality does.

A Checklist of Lessons Learned

1. You should regularly measure the importance of each issue in the eyes of your customers as well as satisfaction with your performance in meeting their needs.

2. You should not just attack areas where the satisfaction scores are low, but make sure the areas are important to the customer as well.

18 Satisfaction vs. Excellence vs. Loyalty

"A discovery by Xerox shattered conventional wisdom: Its totally satisfied customers were six times more likely to repurchase Xerox products over the next 18 months than its satisfied customers. The implications were profound: Merely satisfying customers who have the freedom to make choices is not enough to keep them loyal. The only truly loyal customers are totally satisfied customers."[1]

How Do I Decide What Customer Satisfaction Scale to Use?

Customer *Satisfaction* is a misnomer. Think about what it takes to be satisfied. Suppose two consumers, we will call them Dick and Jane, both go out to a restaurant. Dick goes to the nearest fast-food restaurant, while Jane goes to one of the finest restaurants in town. What would it mean to say that they were both "satisfied," or even "very satisfied?" Obviously, they had very different experiences, and yet, Dick and Jane may both have given the same rating on their customer-satisfaction surveys. In what sense were their experiences equal?

The issue is "excellence" is a more discriminating scale. If Dick and Jane were both asked to rate their dining experiences on an excellence scale, they would likely generate different scores. A scale market researchers often use is "Excellent – Very Good – Good – Fair – Poor." Admittedly, this scale is not balanced. There are more positive scores than negative. This is done deliberately because most companies do fairly well in customer satisfaction. The companies want to discriminate between different levels of satisfaction. A more balanced scale would not accomplish that as well as this scale does. (Admittedly, the authors are contrarians on this issue. Many marketing research textbooks recommend a "balanced" scale.)

The graph below illustrates some of the differences between using satisfaction scales and an excellence scale. Note that "Very Satisfied" and especially "Somewhat Satisfied" could mean almost anything on the excellence scale. These ratings are not very discriminating. On the other hand, an "Excellent" rating represents almost assuredly a "Very Satisfied" experience. The excellence scale is much more discriminating, and that is what you desire from a rating scale: the ability to discriminate between different levels of performance.

Why Shouldn't I Combine All Positive Ratings?

We have also seen many companies that combine all positive responses into one "Satisfied" class. The second graph illustrates the fallacy inherent in such actions. These data are adapted from Ray Kordupleski, formerly of AT&T. The data show how loyal customers were. Who stayed with AT&T after deregulation in the early 1980s, based upon their customer-satisfaction ratings?

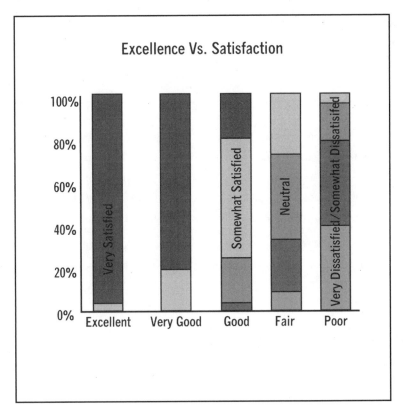

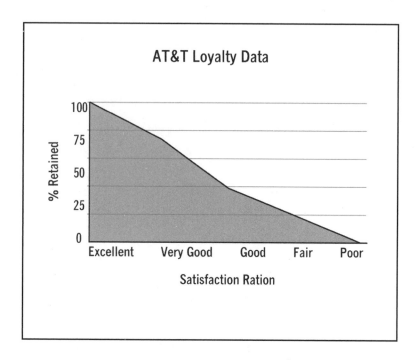

As you can see, even when the customer rated AT&T's long-distance service "Very Good," about 25% of the customers walked. If you look at data from those who rated the service "Good," almost two out of three customers left AT&T. Does it look legitimate, given these data, to combine the top three positive categories? Obviously, not all of these customers were "satisfied."

The goal is to score in the "top box"—to score "Excellent" with your product or service. This is the best way to ensure loyal customers when they have choice.

A Checklist of Lessons Learned

1. The goal of measuring customer satisfaction is to be able to discriminate those things that create loyal customers.

2. Excellence scales do a better job of discriminating performance than satisfaction scales do.

3. Combining positive customer satisfaction score categories is fallacious; you should strive to be "top box" on your survey.

19 How Do I Know Who Is Doing the Best?

"Customers do not buy products or services so much as they buy expectations."[1]

In many of the companies, awards are given to the divisions or departments that score the best on customer-satisfaction surveys. While the desire to encourage good performance is laudable, we hope to convince you in this chapter that these comparisons between divisions, geographic territories, or departments are ill-founded. The comparisons are based upon the idea that, all other things being equal, the higher customer-satisfaction scores indicate superior performance on the part of the associated employees and staff. Unfortunately, this is rarely the case. We would argue that each department should be compared to its past performance, with the department that improves the most being given the "Chairman's Award" or the equivalent.

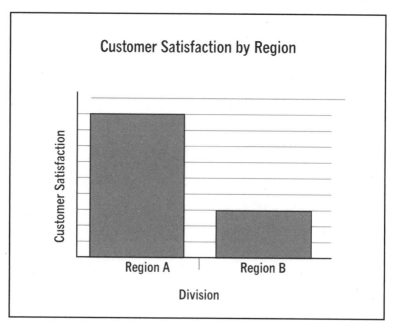

Let's look at some comparative data. For one company that we studied (that will remain nameless) there was little or no competition for a number of years. The customer-satisfaction data for two of the geographic regions in this company are shown in the graph on the previous page. Obviously, Region A must be doing better! They should be given the "Chairman's Award!" What could be the problem with this strategy?

Within a couple of years, there were two major competitors to this company. They began to survey competitors' customers—a practice that is highly recommended by the authors! The results are shown below.

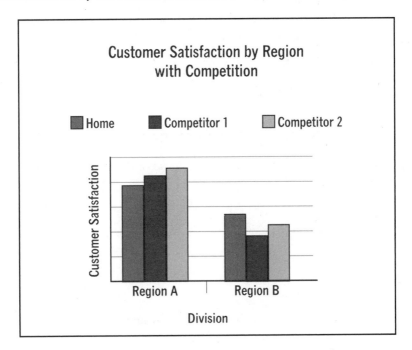

Now what would you conclude, assuming all score differences are statistically significant? Region A has the higher score, but is behind the competition! Region B has the lower score, but is beating the competition! Does this really happen? All the time! There are cultural and regional differences in the tendencies of customers to give praise or to find fault. In this age of global companies, this problem is especially prevalent as one executes a survey from country to country. For example, we have seen results such as these for different regions within Northern California, so it is no surprise that such geographic tendencies can occur across the country or the world.

In this case, Region B was performing better, but had customers who were tougher graders, as a matter of culture or geographical variance. This type of difference can occur based upon time of day, or any other factor that violates the assumption that "all other factors are equal." This assumption is rarely, if ever, true when comparing divisions within a company that has customers in multiple locations.

What should you do? Ask both Region A and Region B to improve their performance. Compare their scores within the same region from quarter to quarter or year to year. Try NOT to compare across regions, as all other factors are NOT equal.

A Checklist of Lessons Learned

1. Where there are cultural, geographical or other differences between customers "all things are NOT created equal," i.e., there are differences in the tendencies to use different parts of your rating scale.

2. Divisions, departments, or geographic regions should each be asked to improve customer satisfaction over time, but NOT be compared to each other. Such comparisons gloss over the cultural differences outlined in #1 above.

3. Regional differences abound within a state in the U.S., so they abound in worldwide comparisons as well.

20 Is Customer Satisfaction Enough?

"I may be 'satisfied', but I'm not happy!"[1]

Does Higher Customer Satisfaction Necessarily Mean More Sales?

In brief, the answer is "No!" You must do more than merely drive customer satisfaction scores up. As an illustration, consider the Cadillac Brougham of the 1980s. The design of this automobile had few significant changes, if any, from 1978 through 1992. The result? The people who loved that car kept buying it, through several lifetimes of automobiles (typically two to five years of ownership). They tended to be very loyal. During that ten-year-plus span of time, the average Cadillac buyer aged almost 10 years as well. Customer satisfaction was going up for this car. Those who lived long enough bought several and loved each one. However, sales went down.

Cadillac was experiencing a diminishing, perhaps dying (literally), market of customers who loved its product. Thus, despite the notion that satisfying customers leads to increased sales (as expressed in The Big Equation of Business in Chapter 2), it is not merely the driving up of the scores that delivers sales. You must also have exciting products that attract and please new customers. By the time the Brougham was significantly altered, many members of the original target market had died. The effort had taken 14 years. Even though these buyers loved that car, Cadillac needed to attract a new audience (increase market share) to maintain or increase sales.

Thus, increasing customer satisfaction scores is not enough. Remember, these scores come after the fact, sometimes one or more years after purchase. They can testify to the initial purchase process and design, as well as customer service. However, what you want is increasing scores AND increasing sales. This necessarily means product enhancements and service enhancements to attract and satisfy new customers and to build your brand, your reputation.

As you examine the proposed improvement efforts for your product or service which can lead to higher customer-satisfaction scores, ask your sales and marketing staffs which of these improvements can be used in sales-and-marketing material. Previously, we have discussed using the "Voice of the Customer" to drive customer-satisfaction proposals and marketing messaging. The improvements must lead to the marketing and sales excitement, as well as improve customer satisfaction, or you may not ever see the link between customer satisfaction and sales outlined in Chapter 2 of this book.

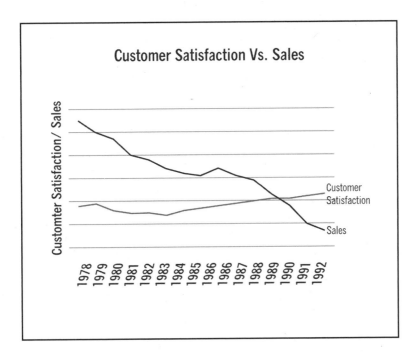

A Checklist of Lessons Learned

1. Customer satisfaction is not enough; you must continue to innovate.

21 Building Your Pain of the Customer Team

A famous marketing research proverb states "Objectives drive design."[1]

Defining the Issue

The first step in forming the team is to determine what the objective of the project is. Define the issue. Why are we doing this? If we had the data we needed right now, what would it look like? If I could throw the final report on the table right now, what would it have in it? If I had that data, what actions am I willing and able to take?

The techniques described in this book work best for wide-ranging strategic issues or concerns, but can also be applied to less strategic issues as well. The customers or targets for the project should be well-defined. Are they internal, external, business, public, or government? Issues where clarity is needed in order to determine which action would have the most impact are good topics for these methods. Other topics that can define excellent issues for this type of work include those where objective data is difficult to obtain and input is needed from diverse parts of the organization.

What do we already know about the issues, perhaps from previous research or from our own staff? How does this project align with the organization's goals? What are the metrics of success for the team (sales, customer satisfaction, etc.)? Whom should we talk to regarding the hierarchy of pains, wants, and needs (customers, past customers, "never were" customers, prospects)? How are the issues different for each group?

Examples of issue statements include:

How do I improve sales training or product training?

How do I improve customer-satisfaction results?

What are the target-audience or segment opportunities?

What prevents our products or services from meeting customer's needs?

What would the customer want most as a new attribute or feature of our

product or service?

How do I improve our customer service?

What do my internal customers want most from my organization?

What can I do to create the most productive employees?

Who should be on the team?

Once the issue is defined, the need for team members becomes clearer. The team should be selected to represent the parts of the organization that may be the most affected by the outcome of the effort, key stakeholders. The optimal team size is about eight members, but team size can vary from four to twelve and still be productive. Teams of more than twelve members can become unwieldy. The sponsor of the project should be represented on the team, but may or may not be a direct member. Team members need to be able to evangelize, to spread the word to others of the progress and success of the team.

The team sponsor needs to be able to allocate money and resources to the work of the team. The team's activities should cross organizational boundaries, and the sponsor needs to be able to assure implementation of the results. One key question for the sponsor would be: What would you be willing to do if the data indicates that it is necessary? What actions are within scope? Politically, who needs to support this effort and how do we solicit that support? Who will need to act on the recommendations?

Team members have a responsibility to participate and attend team meetings. Attendance breeds acceptance of the results and fosters a sense of ownership by the team member. Team members often acquire a "gut-level" understanding of the customer's pains, wants, and needs. The diversity of experiences and responsibilities of team members assures that skills and expertise will be available to apply to any problem. There is an appreciation of each other's concerns, and those of the organization they are representing.

Pain of the Customer & House of Quality Team Building Do's and Don'ts

1. Don't make the team too big.

2. Do make sure each team member (and his boss) understands the duties and time involved.

3. Don't mix management levels within one organization if possible. (It is tough for some people to openly disagree with their boss in a meeting.)

4. Do make sure different parts of the organization that may be affected by the outcome are represented in the team.

5. Do encourage team members to evangelize the results to others in their home organization.

6. Do make sure your sponsor and management are prepared to act upon the results. (Nothing deflates a team more than having their recommendations ignored.)

7. Do make sure the project is well-defined, along with the metrics of success for the team.

8. Don't overreach the issue statement; make sure everyone agrees on the goal of the project.

9. Do make use of resources beyond the team for special requests or data needs.

A Checklist of Lessons Learned

1. The optimal size for a Pain of the Customer and House of Quality team is about eight members. Having too many participants hinders success.

2. Team members and their bosses need to understand that the time commitment involved is not trivial.

3. Define the issue and success well. It will save potential false starts.

22 How Do I Manage My Budget Painlessly?

When he was asked what he would do if he found a million dollars, Yogi Berra said, "I'd see if I could find the guy who lost it, and if he was poor, I'd give it back to him."[1]

The Example

The rigor and discipline of the House of Quality (see Chapter 15) can be applied to selecting which improvement initiatives will have the greatest impact on the customer, which initiatives should be eliminated if one faces a budget cut, and how to allocate resources (time, people, money) among proposed improvement initiatives. In this chapter, we will illustrate this using a common scenario: How can I improve the operation of my technical-assistance center?

The Pain of the Customer for a customer call center has several obvious elements (shown in the table below). For the purposes of this example, we will limit our discussion to these key elements of success with the customer. In your call center, you will want to identify the specific pains, wants, and needs of your customers in their language.

Customer Wants and Needs for A Call Center
The first person I speak to can solve my problem.
My problem is solved quickly
The phone rep is courteous
The phone rep is knowledgeable
My call is answered promptly
The follow-up on my problem is appropriate

After your team has developed this hierarchy of needs, you can conduct two aspects of the House of Quality process simultaneously: surveying the customers and developing predictive metrics. While the surveys are being conducted (based upon the Pain of the Customer, as described in Chapter 16), your team should be building a virtual dashboard of predictive internal metrics, as outlined in Chapter 13. The table below lists some potential predictive internal metrics for our call-center example.

Predictive Internal Metrics for A Call Center
First Call Satisfaction (How often have you called about this problem before?)
Number of Telephone Reps on Duty
% of Calls Where the Phone Rep Completes a Quality Checklist (notify field personnel, ask if call is complete, etc.)
Number of Calls Handled Per Rep
% of Reps Trained in Troubleshooting and Conflict Resolution Per Year

Of course, this is just an example, so neither the Pain of the Customer nor the list of predictive internal metrics is complete. They are just representative.

The House of Quality on page 135 illustrates how your team may complete the process. The customer needs are listed on the left of the House, just as they are shown in the previous chart. At this point, however, we have added survey data. For example, if you look in row 1, under "Importance of the WHATS," the first need (the first person to whom I speak can solve my problem) was given a 5.0 in importance (on a scale of 1 to 5), so it is very important. For each of the six need statements, an importance score was obtained and entered into the House in the first column 1.

As you move your eyes to the columns on the right, you'll find that satisfaction data for our call center and a competitor are entered in columns 2 and 3 ("Our Current Product" and "Competitor 1"). As you can see, we are trailing our competitor in need #2 and #4, while leading our competitor in need #5. For the other three needs, we are equal to our competitor.

We now have entered all of our survey data into the House. Our team, with input from management, can now set goals for our improvement. This is done in column 5 ("Our Future Product"). Note that our team has decided to set high goals for needs #1, 2, and 4, in part because the customer thought they were very important and in part because our competitor is doing so well in those need categories. We have set a moderately high goal for need #6 and modest goals for needs #3 and 5. We must caution you not to attempt to set a goal of improving everything to perfection all at once. Most companies do not have enough resources to achieve that much improvement all at once. The House of Quality allows you to select improvement strategies that will maximize the positive impact on the customer given the resources that you have available. If you have infinite resources to allocate to a set of problems, you probably do not need such a planning tool.

The goals now define the degree of improvement needed in each category, shown in column 6. For need #1, for example, the improvement factor (the ratio of column 5 divided by column 2) shows that the future score is 1.2 times our current score, or an improvement of 20% (approximately—the computer truncates the numbers). We have not, as yet, incorporated the customer-importance scores. That comes next.

Recall from Chapter 17 that it was desirable to find the attributes where importance was high and performance left something to be desired. The next calculation leads to a weighting of each need in terms of that comparison: importance versus performance. The improvement factors in column 6 are now multiplied by the importance scores in column 1 on the far left to generate Overall Importance weights. The more improvement is needed in a more-important need, the higher this weighting becomes. Column 9 shows the percentage of the weights assigned to each attribute.

At this point, we have used survey data (from a survey derived from the Pain of the Customer) about our customers and a competitor's customers, along with our improvement goals, to weight the needs. As a first cut at budgeting, one could assign resources (people, time, and/or money) to meeting the customer needs based upon these percentages. It would reflect customer importance, customer satisfaction deficits, and management goals. However, we will see more powerful alternatives as we proceed.

So far, we have only examined the left and right horizontal rooms of the House of Quality. The list of metrics that our team developed appears in the upper-middle section of the House of Quality. For each metric, there is a note as to whether improving the metric involves raising the number, lowering it, or a target (see Chapter 13 concerning metrics). In our case, it is desirable to increase each metric, except the number of phone representatives on duty. Presumably we would like to strike a balance on that one between having enough reps to do the job without having the expense of too many.

The "roof" of the House of Quality is very important. It captures the synergies and interactions between metrics. In our case, our team felt that encouraging the phone reps to increase the call volume each one handles could lead to some negative interactions. If the phone reps are in a hurry, the customer would be less likely to have their issues completely satisfied and the reps would be less likely to complete their quality checklist if speed were the priority. Our team felt that pulling phone reps out for training would decrease the number of calls they would handle as well. The objective, obviously, would be to mitigate these factors and handle as many calls as *well* as possible.

The middle of the House captures the logic of our team in terms of how well each metric predicts success with each individual need. For example, our team felt that the "first-call satisfaction" metric was moderately strong in predicting success with "the first person to whom I speak can solve my problem." It was felt that some calls could be satisfied on the first call without necessarily being solved by the first person spoken to by the customer. Similarly, the rest of the House was completed. It should be noted that there were a couple of instances where the team felt that improving one metric might hurt performance with respect to a need. For example, completing the quality checklist might mean taking too much time, and having some customers wait in queue during that time (not answered promptly).

As explained previously (Chapter 15), the House calculates weights for each metric. These weights are shown in the bottom of the House. Note that metrics #1 and #5, in this case, are very strong metrics—they predict a great deal of success with important customer issues where we have a lot of room to improve.

As a second cut at budgeting, the prudent manager could assign resources based upon the percentages at the bottom of the House. Now, instead of addressing six needs that represent one hundred pain points or more, he must focus on primarily two metrics! These two will meet all of the customer needs except "my call is answered promptly." (Look for the needs—rows—corresponding to the black dots in columns 1 and 5.) Using this logic, the smart manager would invest in making sure calls were satisfied on the first try and that the phone reps received frequent proper training.

Of course, other issues play a role in budget issues, but if the overriding goal is to meet customer needs, this House can tell you where your customers and your team feel the investments should be made. What if you are cutting your budget? The House can tell you where you can make the cuts while minimizing impact on the customer, as well as what survey scores will suffer. If you cut investment in an initiative to improve a metric, the corresponding black dots will indicate which need statements will have lower scores in the next survey.

The "roof" of the House can indicate such problems as well. If we invest in metrics #1 and #5, for example, the "roof" shows that this will negatively impact call volume per rep. To mitigate that effect, we will need to have a strategy to enable #1 and #5 to increase with calls being handled faster. We might form a task force of phone reps to achieve that goal. This type of thinking leads to the Second House of Quality: the Strategic-Planning House.

Thus, the House can predict Value (in the big equation of business—Chapter 2) increasing or decreasing, depending upon what metrics are improved and how much. Minus signs in the roof can predict some perceptions of value going down, plus signs can predict them going up, attribute by attribute.

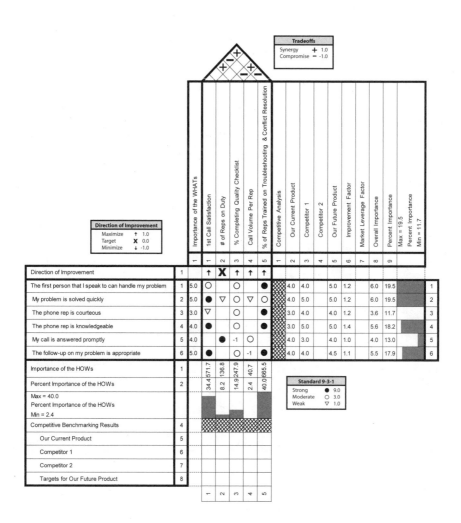

Call Center Example

The Second House of Quality

For the Strategic-Planning House of Quality, a matrix is designed that crosses the metrics with strategic improvement initiatives. In this House, the metrics become the input data (where the "Pain" used to be). An example for the call center is shown below.

The Strategic Initiatives House of Quality for the Call Center

Standard 9-3-1	
Strong	● 9.0
Moderate	○ 3.0
Weak	▽ 1.0

Direction of Improvement	
Maximize	↑ 1.0
Target	X 0.0
Minimize	↓ -1.0

	#	Direction of Improvement	Form Employee Task Force to Perform 1st Call Satisfaction Quicker	Make More Senior Reps Mentors/Coaches for Newer Reps	Hire More Reps	Develop Quality Checklist Using VoC Data	Importance of the HOWs	Percent Importance of the HOWs	Competitive Benchmarking Results	Our Current Product	Competitor 1	Competitor 2	Targets for Our Future Product	
		1	1	2	3	4	1	2	4	5	6	7	8	
1st Call Satisfaction	1	↑	●	○	-1	●	571.7	34.4						1
# of Reps on Duty	2	X		-1	●		136.8	8.2						2
% Completing Quality Checklist	3	↑	●	●		○	247.9	14.9						3
Call Volume Per Rep	4	↑	○	○	-1		40.7	2.4						4
% of Reps Trained on Troubleshooting & Conflict Resolution	5	↑	○	▽	-1		665.5	40.0						5

Max = 40.0 Min = 2.4

Percentage of Strategic Weight   51 17 1 31

In this Strategic-Planning House of Quality, the relationships are developed by the House of Quality team in the same way, evaluating each strategic initiative in terms of how well it predicts success in moving each metric. The calculations are made in the same manner (multiplying the weight of each row by the symbol in each column and adding vertically).

The outcome shows that the most efficient investment would be in strategy #1: forming a team to uncover how to achieve first-call resolution better and faster. The data suggests that to have the maximum benefit to the customer, as much as 51% of your investment should be made in this initiative.

You may be able to quarrel with the specific values we have assigned to relationships, but the methodology is sound. It captures the best thinking of the House of Quality team, management, and customer input in a rigorous and disciplined manner to select among alternative strategies.

A Checklist of Lessons Learned

1. The House of Quality can be a powerful tool in strategic planning.

2. The Strategic-Planning House can be used to evaluate strategic initiatives in terms of the impact they are likely to have on the customer.

3. The rigor and discipline of the House of Quality process can remove much of the emotion in debating what needs to be done to improve.

SECTION TWO:
TURNING THE PAIN INTO CUSTOMERS

23 How to Fill Your Pipeline in Three Steps

Emanuel Rosen wrote, "The more connected your customers are to each other, the more you depend on their 'buzz' for future business."[1] How does this work?

Would you use your pain-of-customer research to fill your pipeline with qualified prospects? Here is a three-step approach that works wonders:

1. **Identify Target Prospects.** Step one is to find a potential market niche that will be profitable. In today's market, customers demand specialists. You want fewer prospects to be interested in you, but much more intensely interested. This requires focus. It doesn't mean you'll turn down a customer who doesn't fit into your two or three chosen verticals; it simply means you won't be actively shaping your marketing campaigns toward them. Evaluate your business. Have you sold most of your services to golf-ball manufacturers, pet stores, and electrical suppliers? Then THOSE are the three places to start thinking. But if pet stores in general don't have the budget for your services, you'll need to look harder.

2. **Prove You Understand Their Pain.** Step two is to determine what promise you or your firm is making to your target market. This includes your unique selling proposition: what you do, who you do it for, and how you are unlike competitors—all in twenty-five words or fewer. What measurable results do you obtain for customers? You need to decide what makes you different than everybody else, and you need to overcome fear of focus: the desire to want to be everything to everybody. People hire companies who specialize. Very few people would hire a surgeon who says he can do everything from tonsillectomies to facelifts and open-heart procedures. When you're in pain, you want a specialist, not just somebody who's

"good with a knife."

3. **Harvest Emails on Your Web Site.** Step three is to create an easy-to-update Web site that demonstrates your competence, rather than asserts how great you are. The homepage of the Web site should have a headline that makes it clear who your target is and what pains you solve. The Web site is the cornerstone of your marketing, and must not be a mere electronic brochure. Your Web site is the silent salesperson that prospective customers visit before making the decision to grant you permission to meet. There should be plenty of free articles with great how-to advice for prospects. The Web site should include an offer—often something free like an e-book—in exchange for the visitor's e-mail address. This e-book should contain valuable information that tells prospects how to solve their problem in general. Then e-mail these prospects special offers that address their pain.

A Checklist of Lessons Learned

1. Find a potential market niche that will be profitable.

2. Determine what promise you or your firm is making to your target market.

3. Create an easy-to-update Web site that demonstrates your competence, rather than one that simply asserts how great you are.

24 Cracking Your Marketing Genetic Code

You can have all the ingredients, but they may not add up to much. When a friend told Yogi Berra that he had quite a mansion, he replied, "What do you mean? It's nothing but a bunch of rooms."[1]

I s your marketing for customers pathetic or genetic? Pathetic marketing messages ignore pain and just communicate the message that "we're in business too."

Here is the *Reader's Digest* version on cracking your marketing genetic code. Before you can begin attracting customers, you need to create a marketing genetic code that is attractive to customers. All of your marketing messages will contain the elements of this marketing DNA that positions you as an organization that cares about the pain of the customers. Here are ten steps that will help you create these all-important marketing genes.

1. **Name your biz without your name.** Create a business name or a Web site name that gives potential customers a hint at the results you can produce for them. The worst possible business name or Web site name is your name. We know, we know, Ford, McKinsey, and Price Waterhouse are named after the founders. But you are not them. At least, not yet. Sorry to say, customers don't want *us,* they want *results.*

2. **Boil it down.** Write a headline for your Web site and marketing materials that describes your audience and the results you produce for them. Do this in no more than ten words.

3. **Name your customer's pain.** What are your customer's worries, frustrations, and concerns that you help solve? This is also called the FUD factor: fear, uncertainty, and doubt.

4. **How to fix it.** Describe your solution or methodology for solving these pains. What process do you follow to produce results?

Offering a proprietary problem-solving process that you name and trademark is best. This answers the all-important question in their minds: "Why should I do business with you instead of one of your competitors?"

5. **The myths.** State the common misperception that holds many back from getting results. Why doesn't everybody do what you named in step 4?

6. **Step by step.** Tell your customers what they need to do in general to solve their problem. Pretend they weren't hiring you and you had to describe the steps they should take for success.

7. **The extras.** List any other benefits they get from following your methods. What other good things do people get when they do what you advise?

8. **Track record.** Elaborate on your track record of providing measurable results for customers. Be specific as much as possible. Use numbers, percentages, and time factors.

9. **Give it away.** Create a Web site with free tips and articles on how to solve these pains. Each article should be about 300 to 600 words. What's a good format? Consider the numbered-tips approach you are reading right now (easy to write, easy to read).

10. **An offer they can't refuse.** Make prospects an offer of a free special report on your Web site. You are offering to trade them a valuable piece of information for their e-mail address. Tell them they will also receive a tips e-newsletter from you. Assure them you will maintain their privacy and they can easily opt off your list any time they want.

A Checklist of Lessons Learned

1. Use a ten-step plan to create your Marketing DNA.

2. Your customer's pain must be a cornerstone of your Marketing DNA.

3. Make sure all marketing messages contain the elements of the Marketing DNA.

25 Less Hype and More Help

Speaking of marketing baseball and the prospects of losing customers, Yogi Berra once said, "If people don't want to come to the ballpark, how are you going to stop them?"[1]

What should you do to generate more leads? You should understand that generating leads is an investment and should be measured like any other investment. The best marketing investment you can make is to offer helpful information to prospective customers about how to solve their pain.

For example, billions are wasted every year on trade-show marketing hype. Take the former Electronic Entertainment Expo (E3) for instance, once the world's largest tradeshow for entertainment and educational software.

While it would be easy to drown in the ocean of marketing hype at one expo, there was a refreshing island of marketing help. What caught many an eye in the expo program was an ad with a college cheerleader wearing a "Hack U" tank top. "At Hack U, you will learn how hackers think, how they work, how they take revenue away from your games, and how you can prevent it," said the ad. "Come by our booth to grab a bite to eat and join us for one of our sessions." This is a great example of using customer pain as the focus of a marketing message.

"Hacker University" (good old Hack U) is the brainchild of Macrovision Corporation (Nasdaq: MVSN), a California company that helps the software industry protect and license software. A Macrovision white paper entitled the "The ROI of Content Protection for Games" was available for those who attended.

Hack U provided timely coverage of the growing threat of game hacking, combined with its real-world impact on revenues. The hacker community's previous focus on PC and online gaming has expanded to include the Xbox®

and Sony PlayStation® 2, further impacting game-developer and publisher revenues.

Instead of just handing out logo pens and other trinkets (hype marketing) to the sea of passersby, Macrovision® was able to engage potential customers in conversations about how to overcome the pains they face.

Some argue that prospects today are bombarded with seminars, speeches and articles that contain generalities and do not distinguish the author or presenter from any of his or her competitors. The answer is a neglected tool: conducting proprietary research on topics of interest to prospective customers.

Macrovision conducted a survey of 9,000 video gamers showing that 21% of console gamers and 40% of PC gamers play pirated games. Most importantly, 73%, according to a news release issued by Macrovision, would have purchased the game within one month if a free version had not been readily available. Thank you for the help. In business, that's something we need all of which we can get.

A Checklist of Lessons Learned

1. Think marketing help, not marketing hype.

2. To generate leads, offer helpful information to prospects on how to solve their pain.

3. Conduct proprietary research of interest to potential customers.

26 The Top 14 Ways to Generate Leads

Emanuel Rosen writes, "...meet the customers face-to-face...don't lock yourself to the latest electronic means of communications."[1]

The theme of this book is that the best marketing for companies is educational in nature. How do you get the word out when you are launching a company, product, or service? Here are the top fourteen tactics that work, but in descending order of effectiveness. (These all work, but are rated from worst to best because we like to save the best for last.)

The Inadequate Seven

14. **Cold-calling.** This should be done by a business-development person, never a principal (nothing says "trust me" like a cold call. A better approach is what we call warm-calling, which is following up on seminar invitations).

13. **CD-Rom or video brochures.** These can be great lead-conversion tools, but they cost too much for lead generation. Instead, stick the videos on your Web site.

12. **Printed brochures.** Again, don't spend too much money up front to generate leads. Instead, create these as PDF files that Adobe Acrobat can read and place them on your Web site.

11. **Sponsorship of cultural/sports events.** Being title sponsor of the right event can have an impact, but it is not the best use of lead-generation dollars.

10. **Advertising.** Isn't it ironic that none of the great advertising agencies built their clientele by advertising how great they are? However, if you specialize in an industry and they publish directories, it is always good to have your firm included.

9. Direct mail. This is the traditional direct mailing of a letter and a printed piece, like a response card. Some have used this cost-effectively, maybe offering a sample or a complimentary consultation. (There is a much better form of direct mail—see tactic #1.)

8. Publicity. While getting your name in the newspaper and trade journals is a cost-effective way to increase awareness about your organization, it doesn't always translate into leads.

The Magnificent Seven

7. Paid ballroom seminars. This is the strategy of renting out the ballroom at the local Marriott or Hilton and charging for an all-day or half-day seminar. Participants should take away a substantial packet of good information from your firm (and a good meal too).

6. E-newsletters. This is the water-drip-torture school of marketing and the opposite of spam. By signing up for your newsletter lists, prospects are telling you that they are interested in what you have to say but not ready for a relationship now. These people should receive valuable how-to information and event invitations from you on a monthly basis until they decide to opt-out of the list.

5. Networking and trade shows. This is an excellent way to gather business cards and ask for permission to include them on your e-newsletter list.

4. Community and association involvement. Everyone likes to do business with people they know, like, and trust. You need to get involved and "circulate to percolate," as one Ohio State University professor used to say.

3. How-to articles in customer-oriented press. Better than any brochure is the how-to article that appears in a publication that your target customers read.

2. How-to speeches at customer-oriented meetings. People want to associate with experts, and an expert by definition is someone who is invited to speak. Actively seek out forums at which to speak and list past and future speaking dates on your Web site.

1. **Free or low-cost small-scale seminars.** The best proactive tactic you can employ is to regularly invite prospects by mail and e-mail to small seminars or group consultations. If your prospects are spread out geographically, you can do these briefings via the Internet (Webinars) or the telephone using a bridge line (teleseminars). These can't be ninety-minute commercials. You need to present valuable information about how to solve the problems that your prospects are facing, and then mention a bit about your services.

A Checklist of Lessons Learned

1. Shy away from the inadequate seven lead-generation techniques.

2. We live in the information age. Give information away to generate leads.

3. Concentrate on a help-marketing strategy that utilizes the top seven ways to generate leads.

27 Your Pain Killer Web Site

When he was asked, "What makes a good manager?",
Yogi Berra said, "Good players!"[1]

In today's world, to be successful, you need to have a
great Web site.[1]

A top priority for any company is to create an easy-to-update Web site that demonstrates your competence. This is done by giving away valuable advice on how potential customers can solve their problems.

Your Web site should be the cornerstone of your lead-generation efforts. The site is your silent salesperson—the one with whom prospective customers, retailers, and partners visit before granting you permission to meet with them.

From a best-practices standpoint, here are twenty-one must-have elements for a superior Web site that attracts new customers like a magnet.

1. **A clear positioning statement.** Tell prospective customers in as few words as possible what you do, for whom you do it, and what results you achieve. If you have a proprietary process or an extraordinary guarantee, this is the time and place to mention it.

   - **How would you summarize your business?**
     This will help you create a written homepage executive summary of your business. Please fill in the blanks and use no more than 150 words total to explain the following.

   - **Target:** We help...

   - **Pain:** ...who struggle with...

   - **Predicament:** ...which makes them...

   - **Answer:** What we do is...

   - **Benefits:** ...so they can...

   - **Why me:** Unlike typical companies, our difference is...

2. **Free resources.** The key to earning your prospective customers' trust is demonstrating that you understand their problems. With that key fact in mind, your Web site should be filled with how-to articles, white papers, and special reports that give away valuable information.

3. **Declare your specialization.** The number-one attribute prospective customers hunt for is specialization, so put yours right up front. No successful small firm is "all things to all people." Figure out who you serve, and how, and put that information on the front page. Be sure to also describe the outcomes you achieve, such as decreased costs or increased revenues.

4. **Mission and philosophy.** According to focus-group research, you should include a mission statement, but keep it short and meaningful. Customers say they don't really care that much about mission statements, but if you can use one to further differentiate yourself, it's a good idea to do so.

5. **Contact information.** Don't make your prospective customers work to find you. Put your phone number on every page. Make it easy for prospective customers to e-mail you with requests for more information or a meeting. And definitely consolidate all of your contact information on one page, including address, fax numbers, and so on.

6. **Map and driving directions.** If prospects ever visit your physical location, then you must include a map and driving directions to your office. This will not only save you time, but is also another reason to have prospective customers poking around your Web site.

7. **E-mail subscription link.** Once you capture their e-mail, why waste first-class postage? Offer prospective customers solid reasons for giving you permission to e-mail them: free reports, studies, white papers, or notifications of key Web site updates. And of course, state clearly that subscribers can easily opt out of your list whenever they want.

8. **On-demand materials (PDF).** What happens if a prospective customer wants to tell someone else about you? The problem with a

beautiful Web site is that is usually doesn't look so beautiful when the pages are printed. The way around this is to offer professionally designed PDFs, readable with the free Acrobat Reader. But don't just offer a standard capabilities brochure; make sure your menu includes a how-to guide or tips brochure that includes capabilities information.

9. **Proprietary process.** After specialization, customers look for a specific problem-solving process or way of doing business. You should create this process, name it, trademark it, and describe it with reverence on your Web site.

There's an old marketing saying that goes like this: "If you don't have anything unique to advertise about your business, then you should advertise your business for sale."

A good proprietary process, however, is never a cut-and-dried industry standard lifted from a textbook. Instead, it codifies a firm's particular method of problem-solving, typically identifying and sequencing multiple steps that often take place in the same, defined order. Furthermore, the completed process should have an intriguing name — one that you can trademark.

What are some of these intriguing proprietary-process names? Here are a few to ponder:

- The I-Innovation Process
- The SupporTrak RACE System
- The NetRaker Methodology
- The Systematic Determination Process
- The Persuasion Iteration Process

Don't worry if you don't understand what any of these processes do just by hearing the names: That's actually the point. A name that is unique enough to actually qualify to be trademarked will also create the opportunity to explain the process to potential customers.

Don't go overboard, however, and create a name that is all marketing hype with no real service substance. Sometimes a line from a movie says it all. Remember when every burger joint had a secret sauce? In the film *Fast Times at Ridgemont High*, teenage workers from various fast-food restaurants reveal what goes into the "secret sauce" for their hamburgers. One says "ketchup and mayonnaise," and the other says "Thousand Island dressing."

Make sure that some *real* problem-solving ingredients have gone into the secret sauce of your firm—your proprietary process—and that the name actually reflects your unique approach.

10. **Seminar and event information.** What are you doing to reach out and touch customers? One of the best lead-generation tactics you can employ is the seminar, briefing, workshop, and/or roundtable discussion. Focus on the biggest problems that you solve for customers. Your Web site should prominently list upcoming seminars (to promote attendance) and past seminars (to promote your reputation as an expert).

11. **Privacy policy.** In a confidential business? Then by all means have a clear privacy policy that states you will never share contact information with anyone else.

12. **Legal disclaimer and copyright notice.** For ideas on legal disclaimers, look in the front on any nonfiction business-advice book published today. You will see language that says the publisher is not engaged in rendering legal, accounting or other professional service and the information is for educational purposes. And protect your intellectual property—your site content and free resources—by taking advantage of de facto copyright laws. Post a standard copyright notice.

13. **Focus-specific information.** If you are a specialist in a certain industry, like healthcare or real estate, then there'd better be healthcare or real-estate information throughout the Web site. (You don't want to

look like a poser or a wannabe!)

14. **News releases.** The Internet is the number-one research tool for journalists today, so include news releases, fact sheets, firm backgrounders, and longer executive biographies in one area.

15. **Public speaking.** List upcoming and past speaking engagements with industry and civic groups. This promotes your reputation as an expert and will also help you garner invitations for future speaking engagements.

16. **Job postings.** Create positive, upbeat descriptions of the stars you attract to your firm. (Some customers will go here to get a sense of who you really are.)

17. **Key-employee bios.** Keep these short—say, fifty to one hundred words. Longer bios belong in the news-release section.

18. **Customer base.** This can be tricky, but it's important. If it is appropriate in your field to list marquee customers, by all means do so. If this is inappropriate, then describe the types of customers you work for in general terms (e.g., "A Fortune 500 Manufacturer of Paper and Consumer Products").

19. **Case studies.** Our focus groups tell us most prospective customers aren't particularly interested in case studies because they believe specific cases don't apply to them and their own problems. A better approach is to take information out of a case study and turn it into a how-to article.

20. **Referral mechanism.** Your Web designer can easily include a feature that makes it easy for someone to refer your Web site to a friend or associate.

21. **Contact mechanism.** The purpose of the Web site is to let prospects check you out and then contact you. Have a device that makes it easy for them to do so.

If your Web site doesn't fully engage visitors, you are not alone. But how do you make it better without spending a fortune? The answer might be right in front of you at any shopping mall or grocery store.

Yes, you can use the science of stimulus-response, also known as retail environmental psychology, to improve your Web site results. The trick is to tweak every page on your Web site to create a stimulus cue that affects visitor behavior. Just as environmental psychology has transformed retail stores like Nordstrom and Ikea, and many other commercial venues including casinos, malls, and now airports,[2] you can immediately use many of these tactics to improve any Web site (not just those with e-commerce).

Face it, most Web site pages are lazy, but it is not their fault. That's according to stimulus-response expert Ron Huber, a principal with Achieve Internet of Southern California. The majority of Web sites never live up to their potential because the interior pages fail to motivate visitors to linger on the Web site and take action. Each page should have a role in persuading a visitor to do something and it should be clearly communicated on the page of what to do next.

In his landmark paper on Atmospherics, marketing sage Philip Kotler introduced the view that retail environments create atmospheres that affect shopping behavior.[3] Today most retail stores like Target, Whole Foods and Victoria's Secret[4] rely heavily on environmental psychology research. Of course, the most-advanced proprietary research studies are trade secrets.

Here are nine common Web site stimulus-response mistakes that exasperate Web site users and hurt marketing results:

1. Frustrating navigation overloaded with unclear choices

2. Inconsistent look and feel past the home page or first level pages

3. Sudden unexpected changes, pop-ups or downloads when clicking on links and buttons

4. Web site doesn't collect names or encourage visitors to provide emails

5. Hard-to-find contact information

6. Baffling layouts that waste space

7. Little or no original content to encourage repeat visitors

8. Outdated information

9. No call to action directing the customer to your optimal outcome

What are the lessons for your Web site? You don't necessarily need a new Web site, just tweak the one you have. According to environmental psychology, each Web page should offer the visitor a behavioral cue for what to do next. For instance, in shopping-mall design, the technique called the Gruen transfer refers to the moment when consumers respond to cues in the environment (named for Austrian architect Victor Gruen). Like a Gruen transfer, each page should offer clear visual stimuli and navigation cues on what action you want the visitor to take. Want to discover a number of specific stimulus-response cues you can use to attract all the customers you need? Visit Ron Huber's Web site at www.achieveinternet.com.

A Checklist of Lessons Learned

1. Use the checklist of "do's" and "don'ts" described above to create and attract customers with your Web site.

28 Five Ways to Increase Your Persuasion Power

Robert Cialdini writes, "People will do things that they see other people are doing. For example, in one experiment, one or more accomplices would look up into the sky; bystanders would then look up into the sky to see what they were seeing. At one point this experiment aborted, as so many people were looking up that they stopped traffic."

To help prospective customers choose you, give them a persuasive mental shortcut. You can gain trust with customers through a proven persuasive secret called social proof.

With more than one quarter of a million copies sold worldwide, *Influence: The Psychology of Persuasion* by Robert B. Cialdini, PhD, has established itself as the most important book on persuasion ever published. In this book, which we highly recommend, Professor Cialdini explains why some people are remarkably persuasive.

The book explains six psychological secrets behind our powerful impulse to comply and how to skillfully use these tactics. The book is organized around these six principles of consistency, reciprocation, authority, liking, scarcity, and social proof.

The principle of social proof states that one shortcut we use to determine what is correct is to find out what other people think is correct. As a rule, we will make fewer mistakes by acting in accord with social evidence than contrary to it. This is why television sit-coms have canned laughter tracks and commercials use man-in-the street testimonial interviews.

The reason social proof is so persuasive is because we are all so information overloaded. Professor Cialdini says his research evidence suggests that the ever-accelerating pace and informational crush of modern life will make automated decision-making more and more prevalent.

"You and I exist in an extraordinarily complicated stimulus environment, easily the most rapidly moving and complex that has ever existed on this planet," writes Professor Cialdini. "To deal with it, we need shortcuts. We can't be expected to recognize and analyze all the aspects in each person, event, and situation we encounter in even one day. We haven't the time, energy, or capacity for it."

How should pain-into-gain marketers use social proof? The answer is testimonials with measurable results, and here are five ways to do it:

1. **Interview past customers to obtain testimonial quotes you can use.** Sometimes it is best to get an outside expert like a public-relations professional or freelance writer to help you with this. You want to drill down to get measurable results. These include raw numbers (increased sales by $100,000), percentages (improved retention rates to 70%, which is triple the industry average), or time (accomplished more in six months than in previous three years).

2. **May I please?** Get permission to use the person's whole name, title, and company name. Simply saying, "Sally from Kalamazoo" or "Bob from Cucamonga" just doesn't build trust.

3. **If you don't ask, you don't get.** Ask for testimonial letters on customer letterhead that you can reprint and use in proposal packages being given to customers. The more you have to choose from, the better.

4. **Tell me a story.** Ask customers who are willing to be your advocates to record their testimonial stories. One way to do this easily is to hop on a free telephone bridge line and have a service like Audio Strategies record the call. This can than be used as an audio file on your Web site or turned into a low-cost audio CD that you can give potential customers.

5. **Be a name dropper.** Pepper your brochures, Web sites, advertisements, news releases, speeches, seminars, and presentations with accounts of individuals who have benefited from your service.

A Checklist of Lessons Learned

1. Give prospective customers mental shortcuts like testimonials.

2. Interview past customers to obtain testimonial quotes you can use. Sometimes it is best to get an outside expert like a public-relations professional or freelance writer to help you with this.

3. Ask customers who are willing to be your advocates to record their testimonial stories for your Web site.

29 Something You Probably Didn't Know About Search Engines

Speaking about the shift from traditional marketing to "buzz" marketing, Emanuel Rosen said, "..this is just the beginning of the power shift!" ...as potential customers have access to many more opinions over the Internet.[1]

Want credibility with potential customers? Better finish high in search rankings! Forrester Research[2] reported that 62% of search-engine users click on a search result within the first page and 90% of users click on a result within the first three pages. Interestingly, 36% of search-engine users believe that the companies with Web sites listed at the top of the search results are the best in their field.

More than half of the marketers (52%) surveyed by MarketingSherpa[3] described pay-per-click ads as outperforming all other tactics. This was the first time search ads surpassed e-mail marketing to a house list, which came in second at 47%.

Following are six simple rules suggested for effective search-engine optimization.

1. **Love those free tools.** Become familiar with the free-tools section of the Yahoo! Search Marketing Web site. This allows you to research how popular certain keywords are and if your competitors are bidding for these keywords.

2. **Make the first words count.** The first 150 words of your Web site are all important for the search engines. This is the place where you should utilize pain-into-gain messages. Make sure you use the two or three most relevant keyword phrases in the critically important homepage introduction.

3. **Consider your target keywords carefully.** Too many sites are relevant for a single word, so pick keyword phrases that are two or more words long.

4. **Don't use just the name of your business as the title tag of your Web site.** Failure to put target keyword phrases in the title tag of the Web site is the main reason perfectly relevant Web pages may be poorly ranked.

5. **Write interior pages with your keyword phrases in mind.** Add HTML hyperlinks to your homepage that lead to major inside pages of your Web site. If you naturally point to other pages from within your site, you increase the odds that the search engines will find more of your Web site.

6. **Keywords are king.** Go to the three major search engines and search for your keyword phrases. Check out what Web sites are appearing in the top results. Visit these Web sites and then contact the site owners to see if they link to you. Links are often possible with noncompetitive sites, especially if you offer to link back (often called reciprocal links).

A Checklist of Lessons Learned

1. To be noticed and found on the Web, you must rank high in the search engines.

30 To Those Who Would Never Dream of Writing a Book

"Talking to Yogi Berra about baseball is like talking to Homer about the gods."[1]

Being a published author is the quickest path to becoming a customer-pain expert who attracts new customers. So why doesn't every business have a book?

Thanks to new technologies, today it is not only possible to produce a professional-looking copy of your book for under $1,000, you can also market the book through reputable sales channels.

A decade ago, there weren't too many options for companies and consultants to get into print as a book author. If a traditional publisher wasn't interested in your manuscript, your only other option was to spend tens of thousands of dollars with a subsidy press or custom printer. And then, without ready distribution, good luck trying to sell the books.

But that has all changed because alternative publishers are able to print both paperback and hardcover books as they're needed due to the bold new digital-publishing technology known as "print-on-demand." Going digital allows books to be produced in small quantities—even one at a time—almost instantaneously. No longer does publishing require behemoth offset presses, hangar-size warehouses, and fleets of trucks.

These alternative publishers have made a conscious decision to offer their services to everyone, rather than give control to an elite clique of editors and agents, as is often true in traditional publishing. While incoming manuscripts are checked for formatting before a new title goes online, alternative publishers do not edit for style and content. These companies do not make value judgments about the literary merit of books. The author decides what the public reads, and the public decides if it makes good reading or not. It is a purely market-driven approach, and allows almost anyone to make a new book available to millions of readers, at a small fraction of the cost of traditional publishing methods.

There are challenges, of course. Because print-on-demand books are not typically stocked on bookstore shelves, authors need to do a good job of marketing through publicity, direct mail, and the Internet. But if you are a nonfiction author willing to be a self-promoter and whose book targets an identifiable market, then alternative publishing may be right for you.

Print-on-demand has enormous implications for writers, readers, publishers, and retailers. Because titles are produced "on demand," there are never wasted copies ("remaindered" as they used to be dubbed in the old days). Paperbacks and hardcover books are priced competitively, with authors receiving royalties of 30% or more. Compare those with traditional publishing-industry standards of 5 to 15%, and the appeal becomes a bit clearer still.

What about the writing? If you can write articles, then you can write a book. And if you can't, hire a freelance writer to help you do it.

A Checklist of Lessons Learned

1. Unlike a brochure, a book is perceived as something valuable to prospects.

2. Going digital allows books to be produced in small quantities—even one at a time—almost instantaneously.

3. New technologies allow almost every business to put out a book that addresses prospect pain.

4. If you don't have writers on your team, then hire someone to write the book for you.

31 How to Stage Pain Killer Seminars

As Yogi Berra once said about his wisdom, "I really didn't say everything I said!"[1]

When you can speak to your customers' pains, they will hear and understand a lot of things that you won't need to say because they'll feel your empathy.

What do April, March, and October have in common? These are the top three months for companies to host a seminar.

To make seminars fill your pipeline with qualified leads, first scrutinize your proposed topic by asking yourself some hard questions. If prospective customers attend this seminar, what beneficial information will they receive? Is this information that my competition either cannot, or does not, offer? Is this information a strong enough pull to justify them spending their precious time with us?

Next, examine how you spread the word. Do you have the right e-mail list for prospects (they gave you permission to e-mail them) and mailing list for suspects (strangers you don't know yet)? Maybe e-mail and direct mail alone are not enough to deliver enough prospects to your next seminar. A key to attracting high-level executives is to reinforce e-mail direct-mail messages with phone calls. These calls also can provide valuable feedback on how prospects view the seminar topic and subject matter.

Event letters or invitations should be mailed or e-mailed approximately four weeks prior to the event. Another e-mail blast a few days before an event can also work well. Give registrants the option to call the 800 number, send a fax or e-mail, or utilize the online event-registration application on the Internet to register for an event. When possible, it is helpful to provide an overview of what will be covered.

Here are some business-to-business seminar-scheduling guidelines:

- No business seminars on weekends
- Avoid Monday and consider Friday carefully
- Avoid seminars in a holiday week (Fourth of July, June commencement)
- Check for conflicting industry events

According to research conducted by the New Client Marketing Institute, the best months to hold a seminar in rank order are:

1. March
2. October
3. April
4. September
5. November
6. January
7. February
8. June
9. May
10. July
11. August
12. December

The New Client Marketing Institute also found that telemarketing calls can increase registrations 5% beyond the registration rate from direct mail. Calling is conducted one to three weeks prior to the event. Many seminar experts recommend three call attempts per contact with pain messages on the first and third attempts.

Typically, only 40 to 50% of those who say they will attend a free seminar actually attend, reports the research from the New Client Marketing Institute. To minimize no-shows, confirmation e-mails are another option to consider. Send an e-mail confirmation forty-eight hours prior to the event. The e-mail confirmation will act as a reminder of the event and provide the date, time, location, and directions. E-mail confirmations can greatly increase the attendance rate at the event.

A Checklist of Lessons Learned

1. To make seminars fill your pipeline with qualified leads, first scrutinize your proposed topic to make sure you are providing beneficial information that addresses customer pain.

2. The best months to put on a seminar are March and October; the worst months are August and December.

3. Telemarketing calls can increase registrations 5% beyond the registration rate from direct mail. Calling is conducted one to three weeks prior to the event.

4. Send an e-mail confirmation forty-eight hours prior to the event. The e-mail confirmation will act as a reminder of the event and provide the date, time, location, and directions.

32 Where to Go Next: Employees

"Beating the drum for top quality scores is a snare. Instead, we should patiently create processes and a culture that make every day for everyone an adventure in pursuit of improvement. The eventual measure of quality is almost incidental – a more or less natural outcome of a continuing, passionate journey."[1]

Have you ever thought of your employees, particularly your sales staff, as customers of management? Henry Ford thought of his employees as customers for his cars. He wanted to pay them enough and charge the buyers so little that his employees could afford to buy the cars that they made.[2] I think we should go even further with the sales staff: We should literally treat them as customers of their company's management. If that's not something more and more businesses recognize in the future, it should be.

Many salespeople are incentivized to sell. They often make a percentage of their income based upon how well they do in sales. A recent *Dilbert* cartoon strip (Scott Adams Inc., 2004) focused on strategies for selling without a sales staff. The pointy-haired boss thought he could reduce headcount by eliminating sales but needed marketing to find a way to get customers to select their products, pay for them, and pick them up at the warehouse. Obviously, a sales staff is needed to meet customers' needs.

How might a company take the idea of treating sales staff like customers to heart? As we described earlier (Chapter 4) there are benefits to following a robust process for developing customer-centric products and services (see the figure below). There is no reason that the same process cannot be used for employees, as we have done for our clients. What we have done in these companies is to follow the same process for developing ideas to improve the performance of employees and sales staff, as if they were customers of management.

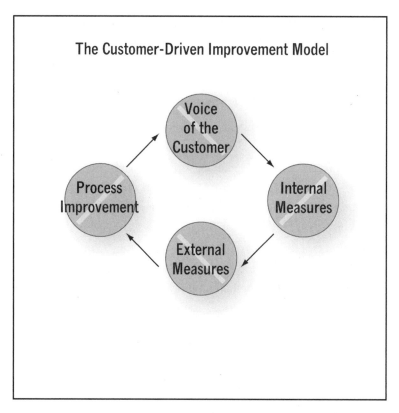

The Customer-Driven Improvement Model

One company (who will remain unidentified) that followed this system makes high-tech products for business-to-business sales. First, the company conducted a detailed "Voice of the Salesperson" study. Management had assumed that the salespeople would want more perks, more money, and more time off. In fact, most of the wants, needs, and pains that were described had to do with reducing roadblocks that get in the way of doing a good job: excess paperwork and reports put in place by management, travel restrictions, and lack of up-to-date sales tools.

Wants and Needs

As part of that study 20 salespeople from around the world were interviewed one-on-one, as is commonly recommended in "Voice of the Customer" studies. After the researchers had generated a list of seventy-five specific wants and needs from these interviews, the researchers conducted—using the language of the salespeople—a focus group of salespeople to organize and categorize the needs. The salespeople in the focus group created sixteen categories of wants and needs. These represented their major ideas for describing the ideal salesperson experience in this company.

A team of sales managers and salespeople met to construct a set of internal metrics to predict success with the sixteen categories. For example, the "amount of time required to generate reports" back to the home office was seen as a metric linked to sales-employee satisfaction. The salespeople wanted this metric to be reduced, so they could spend more time and effort selling. Another example was the ability to link information between different sales tools. Some of the tools required the salesperson to enter customer information multiple times in different tracking tools. Team members felt that this was wasted time and effort that had nothing to do with sales success. The metric used was a subset of the previous metric, namely, "time required to enter customer identification and sales data in sales tools."

Twenty metrics were generated to link to the categories of salesperson wants and needs. These metrics were used to generate a salesperson employee-satisfaction survey. In a very real sense, the sales employees wrote the employee-satisfaction survey; the questions were derived from the categories they had created. In this way, the survey was telling managers what sales employees wanted to say, rather than what management might have asked. The sales staff worldwide was surveyed to determine how well people felt they were supported by the company. Nearly everyone responded, as they recognized that the issues in the survey were *their* issues, phrased in *their* language.

The employee team then related the internal predictive metrics and survey data to the categories of wants and needs through a process known as Quality Function Deployment, as described in Chapter 15. Remember, the most powerful metrics are those than can affect several needs rather than just one.

The internal predictive metrics and survey results were used to generate strategies for improving sales success and evaluated. The survey was implemented again, several months later. In this company, several key strategies emerged that led to a tremendous reduction in the time required to track and report sales progress. The sales tools were integrated and updated.

The result was a 25% increase in sales without hiring additional salespeople! A robust system of metrics, surveys, and analysis had been created that could be perpetuated. Employee satisfaction improved significantly, as the sales staff felt that management was listening to them and being responsive.

Company executives had learned how to treat their sales force as customers of management and management decisions. Management saw that treating salespeople like customers resulted in better service to the customers and higher customer-satisfaction scores.

Treating the sales staff as customers of management and management systems resulted in increased revenue and profits for the company, as well. And that is the mission of the employees and sales staff, isn't it?

33 Pulling It All Together

"Listening to customers must become everybody's business. With most competitors moving ever faster, the
race will go to those who listen (and respond) most
intently."[1]

As you review the contents of this book, consider how to use the information and tips that have been given, whether you are in a large company, a small company, a startup, or if you are a consultant.

Have you learned how to listen to customers with an objective ear?

Do you understand how the pain points the customer or client has experienced lead to building a hierarchy of pains and needs, or the definition of a marketing opportunity?

Can you predict how successful your product or service will be using internal predictive measures?

If the situation requires your action, do you know where you can best afford to make budget cuts? Do you know where you can least afford to cut?

Do you know how to translate the customer data, competitor data, and company data into prioritized actions that are sure to please your customers?

Do you know the most effective ways to reach your customers or clients in today's world? What do you say to them? How do you acquire them as customers?

One of the people interviewed for this book was Frode Odegard, President and CEO of the Lean Software Institute. He commented that many executive-level clients are seeking "breakthrough" products and innovation. Odegard has heard it said that customers cannot be consulted in the process of designing innovative new products. The supposition is that they won't be able to describe the breakthroughs needed and can only give you ideas for incremental improvements.

But for a significant breakthrough, don't you need to address a big pain...make something a lot faster or easier or less difficult?

You need to get the customer to believe that your product innovation can deal with their pain. Perhaps we need a "Pain of the Customer" analysis of the sales/purchasing process. (This has been done by some companies.) Who better to describe that pain, where it comes from, where it is felt, than the customer? Understanding them is understanding their pain in both the open marketplace and business to business. The most frequently cited reason for product failure is a lack of understanding of the marketplace. It would seem foolhardy NOT to ask the customer what pains may need an innovative solution! What our book describes is how to get an articulate description of the pain and how to use that to design products and services that "win" in the marketplace, as well as how to get the message to the customer.

However, the executives mentioned may be asking the wrong question. As stated in the Big Equation of Business (Chapter 2) our goal is to make profits. We can do this by creating value for our customers. But value alone is insufficient, whether it is from incremental improvements or "breakthrough" innovation. We have seen breakthrough innovation that did not sell because the company did not adequately understand the customer's world. At Polaroid, for example, Dr. Edwin Land invented instant photography not once, but twice, using completely different processes.[2] The first time was in the late 1940s. The second time was Polavision® instant movies. Truly a remarkable achievement, but the customers did not want to get their films developed by a special machine at the drugstore. Nor did they want a two-minute silent film. Sony Corporation came out with two-hour video machines with sound at about the same time. Dr. Land's innovative technical breakthrough didn't sell! Dr. Land did not understand the customer's world or their pain in having to go to the drugstore for developing, nor their desire for sound.[3]

What may be required is understanding the customer's buying process much more directly and linking it with the product-design process. It may be that executives are often so trapped in silos that they keep thinking about engineering, marketing, sales, and support as disconnected. The result of this thinking is, of course, that these areas BECOME disconnected. The big equation of business stresses how all of these activities should be connected if we are to generate profits.

Product managers and marketers in the auto industry, the software industry, and the electronics industry, as well as the journalists who write about them, have been stuck on competing in terms of features for a long time. A recent seminar topic at a software-industry council in our area was "What Features Do Customers Want? — Finding Customer Requirements."[4] We believe that this focus on features may be changing, thank goodness!

Some companies have approached making their products fun, not just products with features. How would you predictively measure that aspect of your product design? They have stressed simplicity of use and providing a pleasant experience for the user. Are these "features" or a deeper understanding of the customer needs and pains with respect to electronic devices? IDEO is a design firm that specializes in this type of thinking.[5] Their designs represent a way of thinking about business, not merely products with features. Our guess is that these innovative product designs are steeped in customer research, not just research on wants and needs, but also on the pains and difficulties in dealing with some of IDEO's clients' own pains and their competitors' products.

A Call to Action

If you cannot yet answer the questions posed at the beginning of this chapter about your customers and your company's metrics, get busy. The Big Equation of Business (Chapter 2) lays out the framework for thinking about these issues. As a responsible businessperson, you should be able to describe all the linkages in that equation with data. Few companies succeed for the long haul without complete understanding of the customers and the market.[6]

In this book, we have described the tactics needed to develop an understanding of customer pains, wants, and needs, as well as how to develop and use that information. Put these techniques to use in designing your own systems of internal predictive metrics and management strategies to raise scores and profits.

We will continue to research the Big Equation of Business and Pain Killer Marketing as well as all that the terms entail. We are focusing on employees, particularly salespeople, in our current efforts. The "Voice/Pain of the Employee/Salesperson" is of great interest to us. Our research is focusing on using similar techniques to those described here to understand the employee-satisfaction issues and employee metrics encompassed in the Big Equation of Business, as described in the example in Chapter 32.

We encourage the reader to use the techniques we have described in Pain Killer Marketing to design and sell winning products in the marketplace, delight customers and make money for shareholders.

APPENDIX

The purpose of this appendix is to give examples of interview guides, the "Voice of the Customer" surveys that have been developed using these tools, and the House of Quality from the public domain.

Example Interview Guide

This is an example of a simple interview guide. It is designed to find out what needs and pains companies may have in dealing with a charitable organization. The client's name has been hidden. Note the attempt in the questions to be generic, open-ended, and moving from general to more specific issues.

(MY CLIENT) Interview Guide

1. Purpose:

My name is _____ I am interested in how you and your company think about the opportunities that you give your employees to contribute to charities. Specifically, I am interested in your relationship(s) with charitable federations (e.g., United Way, Community Health Charities of California, Earth Share), how well they work for you, what the issues and considerations are for your company, etc.

2. Warm-Up:

Tell me about yourself and your responsibilities.

3. Current Status:

Tell me about your employee charitable-giving plans and how they work. What works well and what doesn't?

What organizations do you currently work with (MY CLIENT), United Way, etc.?

Where does employee giving fit into your company's plans (i.e., what kind of priority is it)?

How is your staff involved?

How does the economy (9/11) affect your employee-giving programs and your staffing?

What would you say are your greatest challenges with respect to employee-giving programs?

What would make your life easier, or your employees' lives easier, with respect to giving to charities?

4. Analysis Issues:

How do you decide which charitable organizations to work with?

How could an organization like (MY CLIENT) influence their chances of becoming one of those organizations? What do you know about (MY CLIENT) and how they work?

Have you seen or heard of companies hiring third parties to manage employee-giving activities?

Why do you think a company would choose to do that?

What is the advantage to that approach over working with an existing charitable federation or association?

How do you look at the "cost/benefit" issues with respect to charitable organizations? That is, do you think about the time and effort involved in working with them? What about their performance with respect to managing employee-giving campaigns? Is the issue of a "campaign" versus "give to whomever you want whenever you want" important?

How can an organization like (MY CLIENT) present itself in the most favorable light? What would you like to hear from such an organization to encourage you to advocate within your company for them? Who would make the decision and how would the decision be made to incorporate an organization like (MY CLIENT) into your employee-giving efforts?

5.Conclusion:

What else would you like to tell me with respect to these issues? What did I forget to ask?

THANK YOU!

The following examples were for a more complicated example derived from the Workforce Investment Act from 1998 (http://www.workingforamerica.org/documents/workforce.htm), wherein congress and the president agreed on ways to enable those on welfare to acquire job training and skills through government programs. The intent was to reduce the number of people on welfare and help American businesses at the same time. The idea was that a job seeker or employer could find all the resources they needed in "one stop." There are obviously more questions here than could ever be asked in one interview. This illustrates the point from the text (Chapter 8) that all questions will eventually be asked of someone, but not all questions will be asked in any one interview.

The following three documents are the one-on-one interview guides that were used to develop the Voice of the Customer for job seekers and for employers. For employers, there were a few questions that were asked only of those who had signed a contract with the One Stop. In some cases the question refers to "FresnoWorks." Obviously, in cases where the job seeker or employer had been working with a One Stop in a different county, the appropriate facility name was used.

DISCUSSION GUIDE - Job Seekers

Introduction – why we're here, explain interview process, etc.

WARMUP/CURRENT STATUS

1. What kind of job are you looking for?

- Have you had any contact yet with companies you found through FresnoWorks? Tell me about that. (Probe for whether they've interviewed, sent résumés, received offers, etc.)

- Confirm whether or not JTPA client.

AWARENESS

2. How did you hear about FresnoWorks?

OVERALL PROCESS OF USING THE SERVICE

3. How long should [did] it take between the time in which you first come here until the time you find a job?

- How appropriate do you fell that is/was?

- What should take more/less time?

4. Tell me about the first time you came in. What was that process like?

- What was your first impression of the facility?

- What worked/didn't work?

5. What do you do there during a typical visit?

- How long is a typical visit? [MAY DIRECT INTERVIEW TO "SPECIFIC SERVICES" FROM HERE.]

- With whom do you interact during a visit? Ask for each of the following – enough or not enough interaction?

- Staff [MAY DIRECT INTERVIEW TO "STAFF/ORG" FROM HERE.]

- Fellow users.

6. How do you feel about the interaction you have had with potential employers through your experience here?

- How do you make contact?

- Do they come to the center or do you write to them and request an interview?

- How should it happen?

- Are you conducting any job search activities without using the agency in any way? Tell me about these activities.

- Do you feel that you have access to enough companies through the program, or not?

- What do you think about the companies who list jobs?

- What companies do you wish would get more involved in hiring from FresnoWorks?

7. How well prepared do you feel when going on a job interview that's been arranged through FresnoWorks?

- Have you had an experience where you felt under-prepared?

- After the interview, what help do you need? And get?

- Feedback if didn't get the job.

- Help with negotiating the offer.

8. What will happen [happened] when you decide[d] to take a job? Was there anything you had to do (e.g., exit interview, fill out forms, etc.)?

   - People who've found jobs already.

   - How do they keep in touch with you after you take a job?

   - Nature of contacts.

   - Should they? Should they not?

   - People who haven't found jobs yet.

   - Will they keep in touch with you? Should they? Should they not?

SPECIFIC SERVICES

9. Which services do you use? For each service:

   - If haven't used, ask why.

   - What would make you use this service more?

   - Probe for overall impressions and comments on each of the following:

   ### A. Orientation

   - How well did it prepare you to use the services?

   - Was it at a convenient time for you?

   ### B. Training Programs
   #### Quality

   - Can you get training in skills that you need? Please explain.

   - How well does/did the training prepare you for the job you're seeking?

   - What has been your favorite experience with a training program?

   - Tell me about any bad experiences with training you have had there.

- Is there training that you want that you can't get through them?

Convenience

- Are/were the classes offered at convenient times?

- Did you have any trouble registering for the training? What was that process like?

C. Resource center

Quality

- What do you think of the selection of job openings available?

- What do you think of the information that's available on companies in the area?

- What information is there on jobs outside your geographic area? Should there be some? Probe specifically for interest in Central Valley jobs.

Convenience

- How easy or hard is it to use?

- What do you think of the way the information is presented? Probe for paper vs. electronic.

- What other Resource Centers have you used in the past? (e.g., college, high school, other agencies)

- How does FresnoWorks compare?

- What does FresnoWorks do better? Worse?

D. Case management (if JTPA)

- How helpful is the case manager? Please explain.

- How accessible is he or she?

- How do you feel about the advice you get?

E. Résumé Help

- How does that work? Tell me about what you did. Do you draft something and get comments? What do you think of that process?

• How do you feel about the advice you got?

10. Which services that are not available do you wish they would offer?

STAFF/ORGANIZATION

11. Any comments about staff?

• Probe for competence, professionalism, courtesy, appropriate number of personnel, access, etc.

• Have you had a particularly positive interaction with a staff member?

• Have you had any problems with any staff member? Tell me about that experience.

12. Are you aware that FresnoWorks is actually a group of agencies working together?

• How does that affect your experience?

• Are there organizations that should be added to the group? Why?

• Are there organizations that should be cut from the group? Why?

LOCATION/FACILITY

13. What do you think about the location?

• Probe for ease of access, safety of neighborhood, proximity to other things they need to do, etc.

• Where would be more convenient?

14. What do you think about the facility?

• Probe for privacy issues, cleanliness, equipment, supplies, etc.

15. How do you feel about conducting job search activities via computer from your home or elsewhere?

- If you could access job information from home, would you do it?

- How would that affect your job search in general?

- How would that affect how much you come to the facility?

- Would you consider communicating with agency staff via computer? (Examples: filling out forms, exchanging e-mails with staff, etc.)

- How would that affect your working relationship with the agency?

OVERALL SATISFACTION/WRAPUP

16. Overall, how satisfied are you with this service?

- What are they best at?

- Where can they most improve?

- Would you recommend this service to a friend? Why, or why not?

- What can they do to attract more people like yourself to work with them?

- Is there anything that the agency could do that would make you STOP working with them?

- If you're ever unemployed again, what would you do? Use again?

17. What else would you like me to tell them?

DISCUSSION GUIDE - Employers NOT on Contract

Introduction – why we're here, explain interview process, etc.

WARMUP/CURRENT STATUS

Confirm that company does not have a contract with the agency.

1. Please tell me about your business.

- Where are you located? What do you do?

- What are the occupations of the majority of the people who work there?

2. Have you hired people who've participated in the FresnoWorks program?

- How many in the last year?

- What was the last position your company filled with someone from the program?

- How are the new hires from the program working out?

DECISION TO WORK WITH FRESNOWORKS

3. Did your company ever consider signing a contract with FresnoWorks?

- Why did your company decide against signing?

- Who in your organization was involved in the analysis?

- How did your company become aware of the program?

- What benefits are you aware of that your company would gain from having a contract?

  - Probe for tax break, other financial considerations, motivated employees, etc.

EMPLOYEES

4. What qualities are you looking for in potential employees?

- Please describe your ideal job candidate.

- How would you describe the caliber of the job seekers you meet that have used the program?

  - What do you wish they had/knew that they don't?

  - How do they tend to compare with job seekers you meet in other ways?

- Can you give me an example of a particularly successful candidate you've met? What made him/her successful?

5. How well do you feel that FresnoWorks prepares candidates for employment with your company?

- How would you like FresnoWorks to have prepared someone who approaches you for a job?

- What can the agency do to better prepare job seekers to work successfully in your company?

- What would you expect to be different about a new hire that has been through FresnoWorks vs. one who has not?

- What would encourage you to hire more people through FresnoWorks?

6. How do you feel about the number of candidates you meet for the jobs you're trying to fill?

- Should there be more? Fewer?

  - What can the agency do to attract more potential candidates?

  - How can the agency do a better job of screening candidates?

- What occupations are there for which you wish you could find more hires from FresnoWorks?

- Do they need to come from Fresno? What about other coun ties in the Central Valley? (Ask this along with the discussion about computer connectivity.)

HIRING PROCEDURE

1. How do you notify FresnoWorks about job openings at your company?

- Probe for method: phone, fax, electronic.
  - Which is best?
  - What would be better?
- Is there a format you have to use?
  - How do you feel about that format?
- How can FresnoWorks use computers and the Internet to make the process easier?
- Where else do you typically post job openings?
  - What makes a good place for job postings?

2. What happens when you post a job—where does the information go?

- How does that notice get communicated to job-seekers?
- How well does the agency do at getting job opportunity information out to job-seekers?
- What suggestions do you have for the agency on how they can do a better job of communicating job openings to potential candidates?

TRAINING AT THE AGENCY FACILITY

3. Does your company conduct training at the agency's facility?

- Please describe the training.

- How well does the facility itself suit the classes you offer?

- How does agency staff support your efforts?

- How do students get recruited into the classes?

- Would you like to be doing more than you're doing? What is preventing that?

RELATIONSHIP

4. What other interactions do you have with the agency that we haven't discussed already?

- Do you call them or do they call you?

- Too much?

- Too little?

5. How does the flow of information work between your company and the agency?

Agency

- Do you have a single point of contact at the agency for every thing, or do you call different people for different things?

- How should it work?

Company

- Are you the only person who deals with the agency, or do different people in your company call them for different things

- How should it work?

6. Any comments about staff?

- Probe for competence, professionalism, courtesy, appropriate number of personnel, etc.

7. **Are you aware that FresnoWorks is actually a group of agencies working together?**
    - How does that affect your experience?
    - What agencies should be included in the group but are not?
    - What agencies don't belong in the group?

OVERALL SATISFACTION/WRAP-UP
14. **Overall, how satisfied are you with the agency's performance?**
    - What do they do well?
    - Where can they most improve?
    - Would you recommend this service to a colleague at another company? Why, or why not?
    - What can the agency do to attract more companies to work with them? Please explain.
    - What could the agency do that would make you STOP working with them?

15. **What else would you like to tell me about them?**

For the next Discussion Guide (Employers WITH an existing contract) most of the questions were the same as with those without a contract. Only the differences will be documented here.

DISCUSSION GUIDE - Employers on Contract

Introduction – why we're here, explain interview process, etc.

WARMUP/CURRENT STATUS

Confirm that company **does** have a contract with the agency.

4. How will your organization decide whether or not to renew the contract when the time comes?

- How do you measure the agency's performance?

- Who (what title) will make the final decision?

CONTACT

8. Can you walk me through the contract process from your initial contact to the final signature?

- How can they improve the process?

- What worked particularly well during the process?

- How did that process compare with other similar contracts your company has signed (if any)?

9. What obligations does your company have under the contract?

- What hiring quotas do you have?

- How appropriate are they?

- In what ways can the agency help you to meet those obligations?

- What reporting obligations do you have?

- How appropriate are they?

- In what ways can the agency help you to meet those obligations?

10. Have you ever renewed your contract? (May have the answer from "Decision" section.)

Same questions as Q8.

An example of notes from interviews follows. Interviewees not only articulate wants, needs, and pains, but also opinions, target values, and solutions. These are used in the analysis phase of the House of Quality process (Chapter 15). They may be suggestive of internal predictive metrics or strategies.

Job Seeker and Employer Solutions/Suggestions

During the one-on-one in-depth interviews, job seekers and employers often suggested solutions to problems that they noticed in the One Stops. Sometimes these ideas had already been implemented, but the respondent remained unaware of this. The suggestions and solutions are documented here.

SOLUTIONS - Job Seekers

1. Offer support groups for people in similar situations, e.g., house wives reentering the workforce.

2. Point them toward volunteer activities that will offer experience in new fields of interest.

3. Attract more companies.

4. Attract job listings beyond entry-level jobs.

5. Mail newsletters that show updated information on program offerings, etc.

6. Offer access to word-processing software.

7. Have office software tutorials available for use.

8. Have a phone number to call with software questions for people who are in new jobs to call when stuck.

9. Teach basic computer skills.

10. Offer interview role-playing practice.

11. Post a list of sources of inexpensive work clothes (thrift shops, etc.).

12. Write a periodic column in the Fresno Bee with job-seeking tips.

13. Include job-seeking tips on a Web site.

14. Offer loan consolidation.

15. Teach people how to use agency computers to view job listings.

16. Supply employees with the proper clothes for job interviews and working. Help employees select them.

17. Explain why I have to take tests.

18. Enable me to access job listings from home.

19. Give me free access to a computer somewhere other than my home to view job listings.

SOLUTIONS - Employers

1. Visit small businesses to introduce yourself and your programs.

2. Send newsletters describing programs and updates/changes.

3. Have a Web site with all relevant information, e.g., employment regulatory updates.

4. Allow passwords for businesses to have access to special sections of the Web site.

5. Have a booth at local community events describing FresnoWorks and its programs.

6. Promote job fairs for employers and job applicants.

7. Offer instruction on how to post jobs on the Internet.

8. Offer training on interviewing do's and don'ts, and why.

9. Offer courses on employment law, and recent examples of lawsuits.

10. Have a client advisory panel, and publish minutes of their activity/suggestions.

11. Have roundtables at FresnoWorks for employers to meet and share experiences, maybe with a speaker for some of the time.

12. Have a space for the employer's job reference number on all corre spondence.

13. Don't send dozens of people for one job; in fact, try not to send more than five qualified people most of the time.

14. Visit all participating businesses periodically.

15. Visit employees at their new jobs periodically, and solicit information for improving programs.

16. Ask the participating employers which issues to train the job seekers on (survey them).

17. Agency adapts their job listings to my format.

18. Coach applicants to arrive alone for work or interviews.

19. Agency staff asks me what I need from them and their programs.

20. Check with us on progress of employees/trainees from agency programs.

21. Establish relationships with local businesses.

22. Screen the applicants for drug use.

23. If it is required for my job, make sure the applicants can be bonded.

Employer needs statements derived from the interviews, BEFORE the building of the hierarchy.

EMPLOYER NEEDS

1. Interviewees arrive on time.

2. Interviewees dress properly.

3. Job applicants have good manners.

4. Job applicants communicate clearly (e.g., give complete answers to my questions).

5. Interviewees focus on the job interview, not on personal issues.

6. Applicants can work at the location we need.

7. Applicants we interview have the level of skills and experience we require (e.g., education, computer skills, language skills, physical requirements).

8. Applicants can work the hours I need (e.g., shifts, childcare, transportation).

9. Applicants we interview know enough about my business and the job (e.g., come prepared with questions).

10. Treat my time as valuable.

11. Return my phone calls promptly.

12. I can rely on staff members to be available when I need to talk to someone.

13. Help me solve any problems with employees/trainees .

14. I'm not obligated to keep a new hire if he/she doesn't work out after a reasonable amount of time.

15. Employees/trainees come to work on time.

16. Employees/trainees have good attendance.

17. Employees/trainees follow instructions.

18. Employees/trainees work well with others.

19. Employees/trainees care about their appearance when coming to work (e.g., well-groomed, dress appropriately, etc.).

20. Applicants are willing and able to learn the job.

21. People who interview for jobs really want to work here at my company.

22. Employees/trainees have integrity and a solid work ethic.

23. Applicants are committed to stay in the job for the long haul.

24. Contract forms are easy to fill out and understand.

25. Help me fill out agency forms.

26. The information I give the agency is properly processed (e.g., not lost or misplaced, etc.).

27. Contract procedures are explained clearly.

28. Reporting requirements aren't a burden.

29. Any money we're owed is paid on time.

30. Educate me about tax advantages of agency programs and services.

31. Payment schedule for getting reimbursed for training costs meets my needs.

32. Help me network with other businesses.

33. Keep me informed about program changes and additions.

34. Let me know how to take advantage of programs and services available to my business.

35. Ensure the consistency of the services you provide (e.g., I get the same answers whomever I talk to; I get the same level of responsiveness, etc.).

36. Agency staff members are competent.

37. Agency staff members are professional and ethical.

38. Agency employees care about my needs as much as meeting their quotas.

39. Agency staff members follow through on their tasks until completion.

40. Staff members are responsive and reliable.

41. I receive up-to-date information on employment regulations.

42. Keep me up-to-date on interviewing do's and don'ts.

43. Employer training seminars at convenient times and locations.

44. They offer employer training seminars that are relevant to my business.

45. Employer training seminars present information clearly.

46. Ensure that the time, effort, and money I invest will pay off (e.g., the benefits are worth the effort).

47. My job listings are posted accurately.

48. Keep me abreast of job fairs in which I can participate.

49. They send me the right amount of applicants to interview for the job

50. There are no surprises about job applicants later (e.g., drugs, jail time, etc.).

51. Make it clear which job the applicant is applying for if I have several listings with the agency.

EXAMPLE OF A "VOICE/PAIN OF THE CUSTOMER" HIERARCHY

After the "wants and needs" list has been developed, as shown above, then customers are recruited to participate in a focus-group setting to organize the wants, needs, and pains into a hierarchy: an organized list with categories created and described by the customers. An example is shown below from a major industry association.

I. QUALITY PRODUCTS

A. The products are competitively priced.

The price is competitive.

The life-cycle costs of the product are reasonable.

The combination of product, delivery, and price provides good value for my company.

They provide a good product warranty.

B. They sell quality products.

Their products are reliable; they do what they are supposed to do for a long time.

They have a diverse product line, allowing me to have fewer suppliers.

Their product line is flexible and versatile.

Their products are durable.

I can order a "special" without having to buy a large number of pieces.

C. The product design promotes its use.

Use technology that my technicians already know and understand.

The device is secure, both software and hardware.

Capability for remote access to data and controls is integrated with security of the device.

Face-to-face dimensions of the products are consistent.

Different products in the same product line have common elements (i.e., software, piping, overall size, interfaces).

The device consistently performs to the specifications.

The device is accurate.

Their software is up-to-date.

They use the latest technology.

II. CUSTOMER SERVICE

A. I get prompt assistance when I need it.

Provide outstanding customer service; respond quickly if there is a problem.

I can speak to a knowledgeable factory-trained service person.

There is no "red tape" involved in after-market service.

Customer service is always available.

They provide prompt quality repairs.

Their products are easily serviced on site.

They have great technical support.

It is easy to reach technical support.

B. The repair services are reliable.

They do what they say they will do when they say they will do it.

Their repair personnel do a quality job on time.

I can access their production and repair shops, processes and test labs.

The number of people I must deal with is minimized; don't have to repeat my story.

If the unit fails under warranty, I am shipped a new one before I ship the failed unit back.

I can get spare parts promptly any time that I need them.

Quality training is available for my staff on their products.

They are willing to keep us up to speed.

III. QUALITY COMPANY

A. The company has a great reputation.

Stable company that has been in this business for a while.

Manufacturer has a firm financial foundation.

Their customers and my friends recommend the product and company.

Demonstrate the quality of your production processes.

The company thrives on repeat business from satisfied customers.

The company is capable of maintaining a global relationship.

They trust us and we trust them.

They provide quality references (customer lists).

B. The staff is knowledgeable concerning their product line and our industry.

Know your equipment and my application.

Understand my business (e.g., "Know that I lose thousands of dollars per minute when I'm down.").

Know my needs and work habits as if you were part of my internal team.

It is possible that our relationship can be exclusive—so you won't sell to my competitors.

C. They care as much about my success as their own.

Be customer-focused; not arrogant.

Take the time to build a relationship.

Care enough to ask me questions.

The relationship between our companies is healthy at all levels, from technicians through top management.

The relationship is not adversarial (i.e., no guaranteed purchases, etc.).

IV. ORDERING PROCESS

A. The overall sales process is easy.

Deliveries are reliable—when and where promised.

Know what is possible on delivery; don't over-promise.

I can try the device in my application before buying.

I don't have to wait because their stock is insufficient or too far away.

They provide superior post-sales support.

Local sales representatives are easy to reach.

The ordering process is easy.

Changes in orders are easily accomplished.

The ordering and design rules are flexible and not rigid.

B. The sales staff is knowledgeable and add value.

Treat my time as valuable; make sure you have a good reason to call or visit me.

Salesperson is knowledgeable of your products and my industry's applications; they know more than part numbers.

They know their entire product line.

Sales staff behaves in a courteous and professional manner.

Sales staff adds value to my sales experience; they aren't just order-takers.

C. The catalog, web site and marketing materials are user-friendly and helpful.

Sales claims are backed up by data; proven track record.

The sales literature is up-to-date and contains relevant data.

I know what may be coming in the future from this company.

I can easily access information and specifications on their products (e.g., online).

They provide superior pre-sales support.

Application guides, installation guides, and bulletins provide accurate engineering drawings and information.

The sales materials illustrate what differentiates your product lines.

The advertisements from the company accurately represent their products.

Translating the "Voice" Into a Survey

It is recommended that surveys that are used to collect customer-satisfaction data and importance data are based upon the Hierarchy of Needs. An example is shown below. Obviously, if this were to be implemented online or by mail, the scaling and formatting would be altered. These surveys appear longer in this format than they actually are in practice. We attempt to make the surveys as unobtrusive as possible in practice.

Following you will find **DRAFT** job seeker and employer customer-satisfaction questionnaires derived from the Voice of the Customer. These were expanded to include several demographic and transaction questions found in the Results sections. These draft questionnaires illustrate the conversion of the Voice of the Customer into questionnaire format. Please note that the rating scales in this draft questionnaire were different from the scales we eventually used in the survey. The scales that were eventually used were not anchored "1 to 7" scales as shown here, but "Excellent – Good – Fair – Poor" labeled scales. It was felt that this type of scale would be more amenable to a telephone questionnaire.

JOB-SEEKER QUESTIONNAIRE

Name:_____

Address:_____

City:_____ State:_____ Zip:____

Phone:_____ Interviewer: _____

Date of Interview:_____ Time of Interview:_____

Agency Worked with: _____

ASK TO SPEAK TO RESPONDENT.

Hello, my name is _____ and I am calling from _____.We are conducting a brief customer survey for _____ (fill in local One Stop, e.g., FresnoWorks/Madera PIC) to learn more about the experiences you've had when using their services. The goal of this research is to use feedback from job seekers like yourself to improve the service you receive at the (fill in local One Stop).

Let me assure you that this will only take a couple minutes of your time and that this is absolutely not a sales or marketing call.

According to our records you contacted _____ (fill in local One Stop) on _____ (date) to help you find a job/training in _____. That contact and the results of that contact (training you received, interviews you had, job placement, etc.) are the experiences we want to ask you about today. We really appreciate your help in this very important research.

SECTION I — OVERALL SATISFACTION

1. First, I want to ask you about your overall satisfaction with _____ (fill in local One Stop). On a scale of 1 to 7 where 1 is "Extremely Dissatisfied" and 7 is "Extremely Satisfied," how satisfied are you with _____ (fill in local One Stop)? [CIRCLE ONE]

1	2	3	4	5	6	7
Con. to Q1a				Skip to Q2		

1a. Why do you say that? [RECORD VERBATIM]

2. How does the performance of _____ (fill in local One Stop) compare to the expectations you had before you started using the service? Would you say its performance has been...[READ LIST AND CIRCLE ONE]

        a. Much better than you expected

        b. Somewhat better than you expected

        c. About the same

        d. Somewhat worse than you expected

        e. Much worse than you expected

SECTION II — INTERVIEWS

3. Have you been sent on any interviews through _____ (fill in local One Stop)? [CIRCLE ONE]

        a. Yes.............. CONTINUE TO Q.4

        b. No.............. SKIP TO SECTION III

4. How well did _____ (fill in local One Stop) prepare you for those interviews on a scale of 1 to 7, where 1 is "not prepared at all" and 7 is "extremely prepared"? [CIRCLE ONE]

1	2	3	4	5	6	7
Con. to Q1a				Skip to Q2		

1a. Why do you say that? [RECORD VERBATIM]

SECTION III — TRAINING

5. Have you gone through training with _____ (fill in local One Stop)? [CIRCLE ONE]

       a. Yes.............. CONTINUE TO Q.6

       b. No.............. SKIP TO SECTION IV

6. How would you describe your overall satisfaction with the training you received from _____ (fill in local One Stop) on a scale of 1 to 7, where 1 is "Extremely Dissatisfied" and 7 is "Extremely Satisfied"? [CIRCLE ONE]

1	2	3	4	5	6	7

7. How would you rate your satisfaction with the trainer on a scale of 1 to 7, where 1 is "Extremely Dissatisfied" and 7 is "Extremely Satisfied"? [CIRCLE ONE]

1	2	3	4	5	6	7

8. How would you rate the training program at qualifying you for the job you wanted on a scale of 1 to 7, where 1 is "Poor" and 7 is "Excellent"? [CIRCLE ONE]

1	2	3	4	5	6	7

9. Did _____ (fill in local One Stop) place you in a job at the end of the training program? [CIRCLE ONE]
    a. Yes.............. CONTINUE TO Q.10
    b. No.............. SKIP TO SECTION V

10. How satisfied are you with the way the training program prepared you for that job on a scale of 1 to 7, where 1 is "Extremely Dissatisfied" and 7 is "Extremely Satisfied"? [CIRCLE ONE]

1	2	3	4	5	6	7
Skip to Q12							

SECTION IV — JOB PLACEMENTG

11. Have you been placed in a job through _____ (fill in local One Stop)? [CIRCLE ONE]
    a. Yes.............. CONTINUE TO Q.12
    b. No.............. SKIP TO SECTION V

12. How would you describe your overall satisfaction with the job you received through _____ (fill in local One Stop) on a scale of 1 to 7, where 1 is "Extremely Dissatisfied" and 7 is "Extremely Satisfied"? [CIRCLE ONE]

1	2	3	4	5	6	7

13. Was the job in the field in which you wanted to work? [CIRCLE ONE]

      a. Yes

      b. No

14. How would you rate the job at meeting your salary needs on a scale of 1 to 7, where 1 is "Poor" and 7 is "Excellent"? [CIRCLE ONE]

1	2	3	4	5	6	7

15. Are you still employed at the job? [CIRCLE ONE]

      a. Yes.............. SKIP TO Q.16

      b. No.............. CONTINUE TO Q.15a

15a. What happened? [RECORD VERBATIM]

| |
| |
| |

16. How long have you been/were you employed there? _____

days / months / years

SECTION V — STAFF

17. How would you describe your overall satisfaction with the staff at _____ (fill in local One Stop) on a scale of 1 to 7, where 1 is "Extremely Dissatisfied" and 7 is "Extremely Satisfied"? [CIRCLE ONE]

1	2	3	4	5	6	7

SECTION VI — PERFORMANCE RATINGS

18. I'm going to read you a list of items that others have said they want from a training/job-placement agency. Thinking about your last experience with _____ (fill in local One Stop), please rate how good a job they did on each of these items on a scale of 1 to 7, where 1 is "Poor" and 7 is "Excellent." [CIRCLE ONE RESPONSE FOR EACH ITEM]

a. Job-Search Support

	<Poor/ Excellent>
Working with you to help you find training or a job, no matter how long it takes	1 2 3 4 5 6 7 NA
Making you aware of all of your career options	1 2 3 4 5 6 7 NA
Coaching you on job-search skills such as résumés, cover letters, and interviewing techniques	1 2 3 4 5 6 7 NA
Scheduling appointments at convenient times and locations	1 2 3 4 5 6 7 NA
Helping you find a job that meets your needs	1 2 3 4 5 6 7 NA

b. Helpful Staff

	<Poor/ Excellent>
Providing you with consistent information	1 2 3 4 5 6 7 NA
Being accessible and available when you need to talk to them	1 2 3 4 5 6 7 NA
Treating you with respect	1 2 3 4 5 6 7 NA
Having knowledgeable employees that know how to get things done	1 2 3 4 5 6 7 NA
Treating your time as valuable	1 2 3 4 5 6 7 NA
Assisting you with any special circumstances you may have such as childcare, transportation, or clothing	1 2 3 4 5 6 7 NA

c. Useful Training

	<Poor/ Excellent>
Receiving training that qualifies you for the job	1 2 3 4 5 6 7 NA
Obtaining job placement at the end of the training program	1 2 3 4 5 6 7 NA

d. Information and Communication

	<Poor/ Excellent>
Receiving training that qualifies you for the job	1 2 3 4 5 6 7 NA
Obtaining job placement at the end of the training program	1 2 3 4 5 6 7 NA

e. Facility

	<Poor/ Excellent>
Providing you with a clean and convenient facility to do your job search	1 2 3 4 5 6 7 NA
Having enough resources and equipment for all potential users to conduct their job search	1 2 3 4 5 6 7 NA

SECTION VI I— IMPORTANCE RATINGS

19. I'm going to read the same list of items again. While all of them may be important to your satisfaction with _____ (fill in local One Stop), some of the items are more important than others. Please rate the importance of these items to you on a scale of 1 to 7 where 1 is "Least Important" and 7 is "Most Important." [CIRCLE ONE RESPONSE FOR EACH ITEM]

a. Job-Search Support

	<Least Important/ Most>
Working with you to help you find training or a job, no matter how long it takes	1 2 3 4 5 6 7 NA
Making you aware of all of your career options	1 2 3 4 5 6 7 NA
Coaching you on job search skills such as résumés, cover letters, and interviewing techniques	1 2 3 4 5 6 7 NA
Scheduling appointments at convenient times and locations	1 2 3 4 5 6 7 NA
Helping you find a job that meets your needs	1 2 3 4 5 6 7 NA

b. Helpful Staff

	<Least Important/ Most>
Providing you with consistent information	1 2 3 4 5 6 7 NA
Being accessible and available when you need to talk to them	1 2 3 4 5 6 7 NA
Having knowledgeable employees that know how to get things done	1 2 3 4 5 6 7 NA
Treating your time as valuable	1 2 3 4 5 6 7 NA
Assisting you with any special circumstances you may have such as childcare, transportation, or clothing	1 2 3 4 5 6 7 NA

c. Useful Training

	<Least Important/ Most>
Receiving training that qualifies you for the job	1 2 3 4 5 6 7 NA
Obtaining job placement at the end of the training program	1 2 3 4 5 6 7 NA

d. Information and Communication

	<Least Important/ Most>
Having a simple process for gathering and retaining your information	1 2 3 4 5 6 7 NA
Providing you with enough information about a job so you can decide whether or not to apply	1 2 3 4 5 6 7 NA

e. Facility

	<Least Important/ Most>
Providing you with a clean and convenient facility to do your job search	1 2 3 4 5 6 7 NA
Having enough resources and equipment for all potential users to conduct their job search	1 2 3 4 5 6 7 NA

SECTION VIII — WRAP-UP

20. How valuable would you rate _____ (fill in local One Stop) in terms of being worth the time and effort involved in getting the job you want? Please use a scale of 1 to 7, where 1 is "Not Valuable At All" and 7 is "Extremely Valuable." [CIRCLE ONE]

1	2	3	4	5	6	7

21. How likely would you be to use _____ (fill in local One Stop) again if you were out of work or wanted additional job training? Please use a scale of 1 to 7, where 1 is "Not At All Likely" and 7 is "Extremely Likely." [CIRCLE ONE]

1	2	3	4	5	6	7

22. How likely would you be to recommend _____ (fill in local One Stop) to a friend who was out of work or wanted additional job training? Please use a scale of 1 to 7, where 1 is "Not At All Likely" and 7 is "Extremely Likely." [CIRCLE ONE]

1	2	3	4	5	6	7

23. How does _____ (fill in local One Stop) compare to other agencies that help you find a job? Would you say _____ (fill in local One Stop) is... [READ LIST AND CIRCLE ONE]

a. Much Better

b. Somewhat Better

c. About the Same

d. Somewhat Worse

e. Much Worse

24. How does _____ (fill in local One Stop) compare to finding a job through the newspaper? Would you say _____ (fill in local One Stop) is... [READ LIST AND CIRCLE ONE]

a. Much Better

b. Somewhat Better

c. About the Same

d. Somewhat Worse

e. Much Worse

25. What could _____ (fill in local One Stop) do to improve their services for you? [RECORD VERBATIM]

Thank you!

EMPLOYER QUESTIONNAIRE

Name:_____

Address:_____

City:_____ State:_____ Zip:_____

Phone:_____ Interviewer: _____

Date of Interview:_____ Time of Interview:_____

Agency Worked with: _____

ASK TO SPEAK TO RESPONDENT.

Hello, my name is _____ and I am calling from _____. We are conducting a brief customer survey for _____ (Fill in local One Stop, eg: FresnoWorks/Madera PIC) to learn more about your experiences in working with them. The goal of this research is to use feedback from employers like yourself to improve the service you receive at the _____ (fill in local One Stop).

Let me assure you that this will only take a couple minutes of your time and that this is absolutely not a sales or marketing call.

According to our records, you contacted _____ (fill in local One Stop) on _____ (date) to help you find employees. That contact and the results of that contact (applicants you were sent, experience with agency staff, etc.) are the experiences we want to ask you about today. We really appreciate your help in this very important research.

1. First, I want to ask you about your overall satisfaction with _____ (fill in local One Stop). On a scale of 1 to 7, where 1 is "Extremely Dissatisfied" and 7 is "Extremely Satisfied," how satisfied are you with _____ (fill in local One Stop)? [CIRCLE ONE]

1	2	3	4	5	6	7
Con. to Q1a				Skip to Q2		

1a. Why do you say that? [RECORD VERBATIM]

2. How does the performance of _____ (fill in local One Stop) compare to the expectations you had before you started using the service? Would you say its performance has been...[READ LIST AND CIRCLE ONE]

        a. Much better than you expected

        b. Somewhat better than you expected

        c. About the same

        d. Somewhat worse than you expected

        e. Much worse than you expected

PERFORMANCE RATINGS

3. I'm going to read you a list of items that other employers have said they want from a job-placement agency. Thinking about your last experience with (fill in local One Stop), please rate how they performed on each of these items on a scale of 1 to 7, where 1 is "Poor" and 7 is "Excellent." [CIRCLE ONE RESPONSE FOR EACH ITEM]

a. Employee Qualities

	\<Poor/ Excellent\>
Providing applicants that match the job you're trying to fill	1 2 3 4 5 6 7 NA
Completing adequate screening and background checks on the applicants they send	1 2 3 4 5 6 7 NA
Providing candidates that display a solid work ethic	1 2 3 4 5 6 7 NA
Providing candidates that have the level of skill and experience you require	1 2 3 4 5 6 7 NA

b. Well-Run Organization

	\<Poor/ Excellent\>
Giving you up-to-date information	1 2 3 4 5 6 7 NA
Having competent staff members who know what they're doing	1 2 3 4 5 6 7 NA
Being accessible and available when you need to talk to them	1 2 3 4 5 6 7 NA
Returning your phone calls promptly	1 2 3 4 5 6 7 NA
Following through on tasks until completion	1 2 3 4 5 6 7 NA
Having staff members who try to understand my business	1 2 3 4 5 6 7 NA
Following up or checking-in with you periodically	1 2 3 4 5 6 7 NA

c. Support Services

	\<Poor/ Excellent\>
Having reasonable, workable internal procedures (e.g., reporting requirements, payment schedules, contract procedures, etc.)	1 2 3 4 5 6 7 NA
Keeping you informed of employment rules and regulations	1 2 3 4 5 6 7 NA
Offering employer programs and services relevant to your business	1 2 3 4 5 6 7 NA

IMPORTANCE RATINGS

4. I'm going to read the same list of items again. While all of them may be important to your satisfaction with _____ (fill in local One Stop), some of the items are more important than others. Please rate the importance of these items to you on a scale of 1 to 7 where 1 is "Least Important" and 7 is "Most Important." [CIRCLE ONE RESPONSE FOR EACH ITEM]

a. Employee Qualities

	<Least Important/ Most Important>
Providing applicants that match the job you're trying to fill	1 2 3 4 5 6 7 NA
Completing adequate screening and background checks on the applicants they send	1 2 3 4 5 6 7 NA
Providing candidates that display a solid work ethic	1 2 3 4 5 6 7 NA
Providing candidates that have the level of skill and experience you require	1 2 3 4 5 6 7 NA

b. Well-Run Organization

	<Least Important/ Most Important>
Giving you up-to-date information	1 2 3 4 5 6 7 NA
Having competent staff members who know what they're doing	1 2 3 4 5 6 7 NA
Being accessible and available when you need to talk to them	1 2 3 4 5 6 7 NA
Returning your phone calls promptly	1 2 3 4 5 6 7 NA
Following through on tasks until completion	1 2 3 4 5 6 7 NA
Having staff members who try to understand my business	1 2 3 4 5 6 7 NA
Following up or checking-in with you periodically	1 2 3 4 5 6 7 NA

c. Support Services

	<Least Important/ Most Important>
Having reasonable, workable internal procedures (e.g., reporting requirements, payment schedules, contract procedures, etc.)	1 2 3 4 5 6 7 NA
Keeping you informed of employment rules and regulations	1 2 3 4 5 6 7 NA
Offering employer programs and services relevant to your business	1 2 3 4 5 6 7 NA

5. How valuable would you rate _____ (fill in local One Stop) in terms of being worth the cost and effort involved in acquiring good employees? Please use a scale of 1 to 7, where 1 is "Not Valuable At All" and 7 is "Extremely Valuable." [CIRCLE ONE]

1	2	3	4	5	6	7

6. How likely would you be to use _____ (fill in local One Stop) again when you are looking for employees? Please use a scale of 1 to 7, where 1 is "Not At All Likely" and 7 is "Extremely Likely." [CIRCLE ONE]

1	2	3	4	5	6	7

7. How likely would you be to recommend _____ (fill in local One Stop) to a colleague who is looking for employees? Please use a scale of 1 to 7, where 1 is "Not At All Likely" and 7 is "Extremely Likely." [CIRCLE ONE]

1	2	3	4	5	6	7

8. How does _____ (fill in local One Stop) compare to other methods of finding employees? Compared to other agencies, would you say (fill in local One Stop) is... [READ LIST AND CIRCLE ONE]

> **a.** Much Better
>
> **b.** Somewhat Better
>
> **c.** About the Same
>
> **d.** Somewhat Worse
>
> **e.** Much Worse

9. How does _____ (fill in local One Stop) compare to finding employees by placing an ad in the newspaper? Would you say _____ (fill in local One Stop) is... [READ LIST AND CIRCLE ONE]

> **a.** Much Better
>
> **b.** Somewhat Better
>
> **c.** About the Same
>
> **d.** Somewhat Worse
>
> **e.** Much Worse

10. What could _____ (fill in local One Stop) do to improve their services for you? [RECORD VERBATIM]

Thank you!

House of Quality Metrics

What follows are examples of internal predictive metrics that were developed for Houses of Quality (see Chapter 13). Recall that the metrics must meet a rigorous set of criteria to be used in a House of Quality.

The following two lists of internal metrics represent hours of development by the two QFD teams in Fresno and Stanislaus counties. These measures meet the criteria described in the text (predictive of, to satisfying needs, measurable, controllable, etc.).

Job Seeker Measures for House of Quality

1. Percentage of contacts returned within twenty-four hours—these could be in person, by phone, by e-mail, or any other method. Could be measured by having staff voluntarily and anonymously turn in data one week per month, or something similar. The idea would be to be more available and accessible. This measure would be predictive of some of the staff attitude and job-search needs as well.

2. Length of time in system (JTPA from forms, others look at incoming forms and do follow-up). The idea would be that the strategies that result in shortening the job-seeker's time in the system would lead to satisfaction, e.g., find me a job quickly, etc.

3. Does job match preference code (percentage that match in hundredths place; others —greeters form plus follow-up survey)? The idea is for people to get training in the field that they prefer.

4. Training-related placement (percentage from the JTPA placement documents where job matches training code) — as above, the job they get should be related to the training they received.

5. Percentage in orientation training (job-search workshop + Central Valley Professionals = numerator; number in door = denominator) — The idea is that most of the people coming in the door (greeted)

should be made aware of what options are available to them.

6. Percentage of the week we are open (number of hours open divided by 168) — the idea is that we should be open evenings and weekends to be accessible, available, and have convenient appointments.

7. Day of initial interview to day the file comes back to the caseworker = elapsed time — this has been a source of delay for JTPA cases where the job-seeker does not know their status.

8. Percentage of staff trained in "considerate/respectful" behaviors and the importance of keeping data up-to-date — this should alleviate some complaints and lead to higher satisfaction.

9. Employee Job-Satisfaction Index — addresses many customer needs. The QFD team will develop a ten-question job-satisfaction questionnaire, to be administered anonymously at regular intervals. The idea is that driving up employee satisfaction will result in higher customer satisfaction.

10. Percentage of staff cross-trained on other functions and agencies (particularly those who work reception) — the idea would lead to more consistent and reliable information being provided to the customer, requiring that fewer people need to be contacted. This will also need to be done fairly frequently to keep the cross-training up-to-date.

11. Number of referrals to other agencies and services (transportation, PG&E, credit counselors, professional counseling, childcare, eldercare, food stamps, emergency rent services, health services, etc.) — the idea is that we should be aware of other programs and services that the job seekers may be eligible for and from which they can benefit. More referrals will mean happier customers.

12. Caseload enrollment reconciliation report (percentage employed 90 days after completion) — this would mean that the training resulted in employment.

13. Job-Seekers Peer Group (Job Club) percentage attendees placed

— a chance to meet and learn from others "in the same boat," but it should lead to a better chance of getting hired.

14. Percentage of Peer Group doing labor market/career explorations (phone — with care and respect for time, Internet, mail, other?) Motivated job seekers will try to learn more about the career they are pursuing. This may provide opportunities for résumé-building as well as learning.

15. Number of hits on career-development Web site. Should be a good measure of activity and usefulness of the information on the Web site. More hits should mean generally greater satisfaction.

16. Number of people getting orientation-appointment documentation. This appointment is set up by the greeter. The documentation will be designed to tell them several important things about their options and expected behaviors (e.g., make appointments and show up on time, etc.). More people means getting more information out into the community we are trying to serve.

17. Number of greeter forms divided by number of working phones — how many job seekers per phone? Try to lower the number by having more working phones.

18. Number of greeter forms divided by number of working computers — same logic.

19. Number of greeter forms divided by number of "other" equipment (fax machines, typewriters, copiers) — same logic.

Employer Measurements

1. Percentage of customers with good attendance during training — this will predict the quality of customers referred to the employers by the One Stop.

2. Job-readiness index — this will measure staff's opinion of a customer's likelihood of being a quality employee by looking at issues that gen-

erally cause employees to lose their jobs, such as childcare and transportation.

3. Percentage of employers visited per year for those with new job orders will assist in a more accurate match of applicant to jobs, since staff will better understand the employer's place of business.

4. Percentage of unfilled job orders where there is follow-up every two weeks will check to make sure the job is available and whether staff are sending eligible applicants and whether the staff needs to be of more assistance.

5. Percentage of employer phone calls returned within twenty-four hours will determine the accessibility and responsiveness of staff.

6. Percentage of placements with follow-up within ninety days. (This is beyond the routine follow-up to determine employer satisfaction with the new employee, whether issues need to be resolved and whether there is something else staff can do to help.)

7. Percentage of letters sent out within five days of a closed job order as a thank you for hiring the customer, available services after hiring, and preferred method of communication.

8. Time from job order to placements.

9. Percentage of OJT monitoring completed every thirty days.

10. Percentage of checks mailed to employers within thirty to forty days

11. Number of businesses proactively contacted within each quarter with supportive services information.

12. Time elapsed from job order to site visit for those who agree to a visit (excludes job orders taken within last thirty days).

13. Length of time a job order is in the system.

Example of a House of Quality

What follows is another detailed example of the House of Quality (chapter 15) from the employer data shown above.

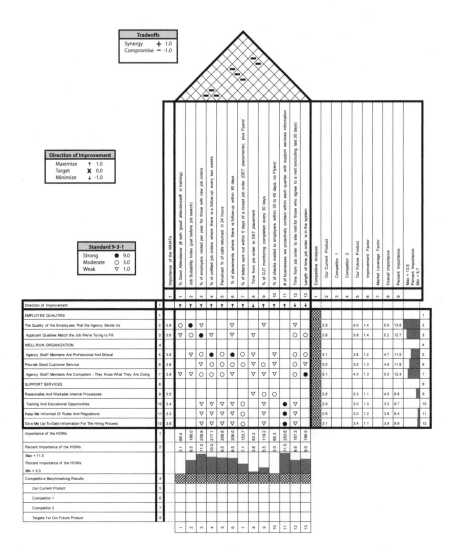

Fresno County Employers Call Center Example

NOTES

1 Are You Into Pain?

[1] "Neural Predictors of Purchases," Neuron Magazine, January 2007

2 The Big Equation of Business

[1] From a lecture at American Marketing Association meeting in Dallas in 1996 entitled "Creating Superior Customer Value"

[2] http://inventors.about.com/od/fstartinventions/a/Fuel_Cells.htm

[3] See references at the end of this book.

[4] See "Creating Superior Customer Value" by Bradley T. Gale in the references.

3 The Small-Town-Movie Theater Example

[1] *The Yogi Book*, p.16

4 Stale Popcorn into Fresh Popcorn

[1] "In Strategic Planning You Get What You Measure" by Robert Bradford— http://ezinearticles.com/?You-Get-What-You-Measure-in-Strategic-Planning&id=606829

5 Who Else Wants to Turn Client Pain into Marketing Gain?

[1] *The Yogi Book*, p. 102

[2] Bartlett, June 1996, McKinsey & Co., *Harvard Business Review*

6 How to Attract All the Customers You Need

[1] *Southwest Airlines Spirit*, March 2005.

[2] *The New York Times*, November 15, 2001.

[3] *ZweigWhite's 2003 Marketing Survey of A/E/P & Environmental Consulting Firms.*

7 Why Worry About the Pain of the Customer?

[1] *The PIMS Principles*, p. 107

[2] *The PIMS Principles*, p. 1

8 Collect the Pain of the Customer

[1] http://www.pdma.org/visions/apr01/growth_forum.html

[2] 15. http://www.quality.nist.gov/Improvement_Act.htm

[3] See Akao reference at the end of the book.

[4] *Harvard Business Review*, May 1, 1988

[5] Griffin, Abbie and John R. Hauser, "The Voice of the Customer," **Marketing Science**, Winter, 1993—Volume 12, No. 1

[6] Griffin, Abbie and John R. Hauser, "The Voice of the Customer," **Marketing Science**, Winter, 1993 - Volume 12, No. 1

9 Use the Pain of the Customer to Write Value Propositions

[1] *The Yogi Book*, p. 107

[2] *Managing Customer Value*, pp. 3–24

10 How to Manage Consultants the Pain-Point Way

[1] http://www.bizjournals.com/extraedge/consultants/return_on_people/2006/07/10/column364.html

11 The $3 Million Leather Seat

[1] *The Yogi Book*, p. 95

12 Changing Needs Over Time: The Kano Model

[1] An old adage, attributed to Diogenes Laërtius in *Lives of the Philosophers*, Book IX, section 8.

[2] Kano, N. "Attractive quality and must-be quality," *The Journal of the Japanese Society for Quality Control*, April 1984, pp. 39–48

15 The House of Quality (Quality Function Deployment)

[1] Spoken as part of "Methods for Management of Quality and Productivity," General Motors Quality Institute, May 1989.

[2] Hauser, John R. and Don Clausing, "The House of Quality," *Harvard Business Review*, May 1, 1988.

17 Importance vs. Performance

[1] Spoken by W. Edwards Deming in "Methods for Management of Quality and Productivity," *General Motors Quality Institute*, May 1989.

18 Satisfaction vs. Excellence vs. Loyalty

[1] *Harvard Business Review*, Nov./Dec. 1995

19 How Do I Know Who Is Doing the Best?

[1] Ted Levitt in *The Marketing Imagination*, The Free Press, New York, 1986.

21 Building Your Pain of the Customer Team

[1] An example would be http://www.upassoc.org/usability_resources/conference/2006/Marine-Driving-Product-Design.pdf "Driving Product Design from the Business Objectives" by Larry Marine.

22 How Do I Manage My Budget Painlessly?

[1] *The Yogi Book*, p. 59

23 How to Fill Your Pipeline in Three Steps

[1] Rosen, Emanuel, *The Anatomy of Buzz*, Doubleday, New York, 2000.

24 Cracking Your Marketing Genetic Code

[1] *The Yogi Book*, p. 57

25 Less Hype and More Help

[1] *The Yogi Book*, p. 36

26 The Top 14 Ways to Generate Leads

[1] Rosen, Emanuel, *The Anatomy of Buzz*, Doubleday, New York, 2000.

27 Your Pain Killer Web Site

[1] *The Yogi Book*, p. 14

[2] See studies like Dr. Alan Hirsch's 1995 article on "Effects of Ambient Odors on Slot-Machine Usage in Las Vegas Casino" and other articles from the past 20 years in the Journal of Environmental Psychology.

[3] *Journal of Retailing* in 1973

[4] Mark Matson, "A whole new ballgame in grocery shopping" March 8, 2005 USA Today

29 Something You Probably Didnt Know About Search Engines

[1] Rosen, Emanuel, *The Anatomy of Buzz*, Doubleday, New York, 2000.

[2] "Interactive Marketing Channels to Watch in 2006"

[3] "Search Marketing Benchmark Guide 2005–2006"

30 To Those Who Would Never Dream of Writing a Book

[1] Bart Giamatti. *The Yogi Book*, inside the cover

31 How to Stage Pain-into-Gain Seminars

[1] *The Yogi Book*, p. 9

32 Where to Go Next: Employees

[1] Tom Peters, "On the Nature of Work," May 7, 1993, newsletter on tompeters.com

[2] *Forbes Greatest Business Stories of All Time*, Wiley & Sons, New York, 1996.

33 Summary: Putting It All Together

[1] Tom Peters, *Thriving On Chaos*, Harper Perennial, New York, 1991

[2] Paul Giambarba, "The Branding of Polaroid 1947–1977" — http://giam.typepad.com/the_branding_of_polaroid_/

[3] Peter C. Wensberg, Land's Company, Houghton-Mifflin, New York, 1987

[4] San Diego Software Industry Council, October, 2007

[5] Cover story, *Business Week*, May 17, 2004

[6] Buzzell, Robert D. and Bradley T. Gale, *The PIMS Principles*, The Free Press, New York, 1987

REFERENCES

Akao, Yoji, "QFD: Past Present and Future," **Proceedings of International Symposium on QFD**, http://www.qfdi.org/QFD_History.pdf, 1997.

Berra, Yogi, *The Yogi Book*, Workman Press, New York, 1998.

Bradford, Robert W., "In Strategic Planning You Get What You Measure", Ezine articles, http://ezinearticles.com/?You-Get-What-You-Measure-in-Strategic-Planning&id=606829

Buzzell, Robert D. and Bradley T. Gale, *The PIMS Principles*, The Free Press, New York, 1987.

Camp, Robert C., *Benchmarking*, Quality Press, Milwaukee, Wisconsin, 1989.

Crosby, Philip, *Quality is Free: The Art of Making Quality Certain*, Mentor, New York, 1980.

Day, Ronald G., *Quality Function Deployment*, Quality Press, Milwaukee, Wisconsin, 1993.

Deming, W. Edwards, "Methods for Management of Quality and Productivity," *General Motors Quality Institute*, May, 1989)

Deming, W. Edwards, *Out of the Crisis*, M.I.T. Press, Cambridge, Massachusetts, 1986.

DeVries, Henry J. and Bryson, Denise, *Client Seduction*, Author House, Indianapolis, Indiana, 2005.

Drucker, Peter, *The Practice of Management*, Harper & Row, New York, 1954.

Gale, Bradley T., *Managing Customer Value*, The Free Press, New York, 1994.

Gale, Bradley T. "Creating Superior Customer Value", presentation given at the American Marketing Association meeting in Dallas, Texas in 1996.

Griffin, Abbie and John R. Hauser, "The Voice of the Customer," *Marketing Science*, Winter, 1993 (Volume 12, No. 1).

Hauser, John R. and Don Clausing, "The House of Quality," *Harvard Business Review*, May 1, 1988.

Juran, J.M. *Juran on Leadership for Quality: An Executive Handbook*, Free Press, New York, 1989.

Kano, Noriaki, "Attractive quality and must-be quality", *The Journal of the Japanese Society for Quality Control*, April, 1984, pp. 39-48

Katz, Gerald M. and Charles Plunkett, "Cleaning Up the Customer Satisfaction Waste Dump," *Proceedings* of the AMA/ASQC's 8th Customer Satisfaction and Quality Measurement Conference, February, 1996.

Letham, J., Slade, P. D., Troup, J. D. & Bentley, G. 1983. "Outline of a Fear-Avoidance Model of exaggerated pain perception," Behaviour Research Therapy.

Levitt, Theodore, *The Marketing Imagination*, The Free Press, New York, 1986.

Nelson, Bob, "Is Your Consultant Doing a Good Job?" *bizjournals*,
http://www.bizjournals.com/extraedge/consultants/return_on_peo-
ple/2006/07/10/column364.html.

Peters, Tom, *Thriving on Chaos*, Harper Perennial, New York, 1991.

Robson, William A., "Growth Forum: Fear of the Customer...a Survival Guide for the
Fuzzy Front End," *Visions*, PDMA.org, 2007.

Rosen, Emanuel, *The Anatomy of Buzz*, Doubleday, New York, 2000.

U.S. Department of Commerce, *Baldrige National Quality Award*, National Institute of
Standards and Technology, http://www.quality.nist.gov/Improvement_Act.htm,
2007.

Wensberg, Peter C., *Land's Polaroid: The Company and the Man Who Invented It*,
Houghton-Mifflin, New York, 1987

INDEX

WIN WEALTH WORTH
WITH WBUSINESS BOOKS

SALES

First 100 Days of Selling:
A Practical Day-by-Day Guide to
Excel in the Sales Profession
   ISBN: 978-0-8329-5004-9
   Price: $22.95 USD

By Jim Ryerson

Soar Despite Your Dodo Sales Manager
   ISBN: 978-0-8329-5009-4
   Price: $19.95 USD

By Lee B. Salz

Great Salespeople Aren't Born,
They're Hired: The Secrets to Hiring
Top Sales Professionals
   ISBN: 978-0-8329-5000-1
   Price: $19.95 USD

By Joe Miller

Hire, Fire, & the Walking Dead:
A Leaders Guide to Recruiting the Best
   ISBN: 978-0-8329-5001-8
   Price: $19.95 USD

By Greg Moran

MARKETING

What's Your BQ? Learn How 35
Companies Add Customers, Subtract
Competitors, and Multiply Profits
with BrandQuotient
   ISBN: 978-0-8329-5002-5
   Price: $24.95 USD

By Sandra Sellani

Reality Sells: How to Bring Customers
Back Again and Again by Marketing
Your Genuine Story
   ISBN: 978-0-8329-5008-7
   Price: $19.95 USD

By Andrew Corbus
and Bill Guertin

Pain Killer Marketing: How to Turn
Customer Pain into Market Gain
   978-0-8329-5016-2
   Price: $19.95 USD

By Chris Stiehl
and Henry J. DeVries

How Come No One Knows About Us?:   By Robert Deigh
The Ultimate Public Relations Guide: Tactics
Anyone Can Use to Win High Visibility!
ISBN: 978-0-8329-5017-9
Price: $24.95

ENTREPRENEURSHIP
Thriving Latina Entrepreneurs in America   By Maria de Lourdes Sobrino
   ISBN: 978-0-8329-5007-0
   Price: $24.95 USD

Millionaire by 28   By Todd Babbitt
   ISBN: 978-0-8329-5010-0
   Price: $19.95 USD

From Lifeguard to Sun King: By Robert Bell
The Man Behind the Banana Boat
Success Story
   ISBN: 978-0-8329-5014-8
   Price: $19.95 USD

LEADERSHIP
Why Dogs Wag Their Tails: Lessons Leaders   By Sherri McArdle
Can Learn About Work, Joy, and Life   and Jim Ramerman
   ISBN: 978-08329-5011-7
   Price $21.95 USD

NETWORKING
The N Factor: How Efficient Networking   By Adrie Reinders
Can Change the Dynamics of Your Business   and Marion Freijsen
   ISBN: 978-0-8329-5006-3
   Price: $19.95 USD

It's Who Knows You: By Chien J. Wang
Networking Your Way to Success
   ISBN: 978-0-8329-5012-4
   Price: $19.95 USD

Check out these books at your local bookstore or at www.WBusinessBooks.com

THIS BOOK DOESN'T END AT THE LAST PAGE!

We want to hear from you!

Register your book at:
www.WBusinessBooks.com to receive the latest business news and information.

You can communicate with the author or share your thoughts about this book with other members of the WBusiness community

WBusinessBooks.com is a place where you can sharpen your skills, learn the new trends and network with other professionals.